STAND BY ME

OLLIE M. KIRBY

JANAWAY PUBLISHING, INC.
Santa Maria, California
2014

Published by

Janaway Publishing, Inc.
732 Kelsey Ct.
Santa Maria, California 93454
(805) 925-1038
www.JanawayPublishing.com

2014

ISBN: 978-1-59641-332-0

Cover photograph of a painting by Tom Heslop courtesy of William Pastor, Jr.

Editing and indexing by Michael Farris.

Made in the United States of America

This book is dedicated to all the Veterans who have honorably served our country. They sacrificed so much for our liberty. If it weren't for the United States Military there'd be no United States of America!

IN MEMORY OF

MY PARENTS

Robert Ollie Brooks
(April 10, 1891 – January 3, 1959)

Nancy Eva (Everett) Brooks
(August 5, 1899 – April 5, 1992)

What greater gift could God have bestowed upon me than growing up in a big loving family in Ripley County, Missouri?

The values my parents instilled would sustain me through many turbulent times. Those values would remain throughout my life.

CONTENTS

Contents vii
Preface ix
Acknowledgments xi

Chapter 1   Alabama 1
Chapter 2   Arizona 15
Chapter 3   Arkansas 19
Chapter 4   Colorado 27
Chapter 5   Georgia 33
Chapter 6   Idaho 37
Chapter 7   Indiana 39
Chapter 8   Iowa 43
Chapter 9   Kansas 47
Chapter 10   Kentucky 53
Chapter 11   Louisiana 57
Chapter 12   Michigan 61
Chapter 13   Minnesota 65
Chapter 14   Mississippi 69
Chapter 15   Missouri 73
Chapter 16   Montana 87
Chapter 17   Ohio 91
Chapter 18   Oklahoma 95
Chapter 19   Texas 101
Chapter 20   West Virginia 113
Chapter 21   Wisconsin 117

Index 123

PREFACE

Stand by Me is written as a tribute to people in the central part of the United States (the "Heartland"), whose faith in God sustained them through incredible adversities.

The stories herein are based on fact, not fiction. The individuals are real, not imaginary.

A very old (1905) Negro spiritual entitled, "Stand by Me," was the inspiration for the title of this book. It was written by Charles Albert Tindley (1851-1933). He was born July 7, 1851, in Berlin, Maryland and was a son of slaves. He taught himself to read and write by the age of 17 and moved to Philadelphia. He went on to become an African-American Methodist Episcopal minister.

"Stand by Me" has endured for over 100 years and is still in the United Methodist hymnal today (page 512, to be exact). The first stanza, "When the storms of life are raging, stand by me," gets the message across.

All of us have experienced storms in our lives. They are not always natural events, such as tornadoes, fires, floods, ice storms, or earthquakes, but can also include many other devastating, life-altering events or circumstances, such as wars, accidents, or the death of a loved one. Turn to Chapter 20 (Oklahoma) and read the true story of an 18-year-old American soldier, who was a World War II Prisoner of War in a German prison camp in France. Psalm 23 (Thou Art With Me) certainly applied in his case.

Ben E. King (and others) rewrote "Stand by Me" into a love song, and it became an immediate success. It went to the top of the charts, and numerous artists recorded it. The Tindley original version was recorded in a gospel album by Elvis Presley. Tennessee Ernie Ford and Willie Nelson also recorded Tindley's version.

The scope and breadth of this book has changed many times during the more than two years I worked on it. My original inspiration was the Joplin tornado of 2011, and my admiration of the "can-do" attitude of the survivors, and the astonishing and unselfish response from neighbors and volunteers to those in desperate need, but it evolved into so much more. People from all across the Heartland urged me to write about other states and events.

My husband and I took two different month-long trips conducting research — one in the fall of 2012, and the second one in May of 2013. People were so welcoming and helpful. It was heartbreaking, as well. We saw people who had reached out to share what they had with others who were barely scraping by themselves. It changed my life forever.

As you read this book, please take a moment to reflect on the people who helped you along the way. And pass it on.

Ollie M. Kirby
June 2014
Santa Maria, California

ACKNOWLEDGEMENTS

A special thanks to the following individuals:

My husband of 48+ years, Eldon Kirby, who endured a 5,755 mile road trip and even did some photography. He also helped with proof-reading.

My dear friend Margaret Doty. If it had not been for her encouragement and help, there would be no "Author" after my name.

Gene Corbin, my computer pro. Without him, I am a hopeless mess on the computer.

Michael Farris, for editing and indexing the book. These are painstaking and critical tasks for any publication, and Mike's methodical and systematic approach, combined with his attention to detail, have proved invaluable.

William Pastor, Jr. "Bill" did the photography of the water-color painting for the cover of this book. It was quite difficult, since I had already had it framed with glass covering the painting.

Tom Heslop, Artist, whose water-color painting graces the cover of this book.

Clyde and Donna Stout of Joplin, Missouri. They did so many wonderful things to help, that I can't even remember them all.

Fred and Kathy Mason, survivors of the Joplin tornado. I am so grateful that they would share their story with me.

David Hampton and family of Tuscaloosa, Alabama. They showed us what real "Southern Hospitality" is. David is a U.S. Army retired officer and very organized. He set up advance appointments prior to our arrival (including one with the Mayor of Tuscaloosa). Many thanks to his uncle, John T. Pike, who put me in touch with him.

Jay Jeffery, World War II POW from Oklahoma. His life story of hardship and survival will make you humble.

GOD BLESS AMERICA

CHAPTER ONE

ALABAMA

History

Alabama has a rich and colorful history dating back to 1519 when explorer Alonso Alvarez de Pineda sailed into Mobile Bay. Then in 1763 the Treaty of Paris gave Mobile to Britain. In 1810, Alabama was admitted as the 22nd state. In 1861, Montgomery became the first capital of the Confederacy. In 1831 the University of Alabama was established in Tuscaloosa.

Cotton was king until 1915 when the boll weevil devastated the state's one-crop economy. This forced a diversification in agriculture for the state.

Birmingham, once dubbed the "Pittsburg of the South" because of its steel production, took a steep downturn after World War II ended. Several factories closed. Unemployment escalated. Pollution from years of heavy industry took its toll on the economy.

Cars Fell On Alabama

In 1993 the Mercedes-Benz U.S. International, Inc. (MBUSHI) decided to locate an assembly plant in Alabama near Tuscaloosa. Now two decades later Alabama has emerged as one of the nation's leading car manufacturers. Military and aerospace had also decided Alabama was the place to be.

In 2005 Hurricane Katrina hit the Gulf Coast. Mobile is Alabama's only seaport. The major impact of Katrina was in New Orleans.

Then April 25-28, 2011, the largest single-system tornado ever recorded occurred. Its deadly path extended from the deep South all the way to Canada. 348 people were killed. 253 of those were in Alabama. Less than a month later Joplin, Missouri, was hit by a tornado that captured the attention of the entire world.

Some of the National assistance and attention was quickly diverted from Tuscaloosa to Joplin.

Also, the tornado that hit Alabama was spread over five states, not just one. Small towns in Alabama, of necessity, had to fend for themselves.

In the Alabama subchapters herein, some local people are highlighted and given recognition. There was so much caring and compassion everywhere I went on my trip to Alabama May 19-23, 2013.

My exposure to Alabama prior to writing this book was:

1. A senior high school trip from Doniphan, Missouri, on which we toured Bellingrath Gardens at Theodore, Alabama, a suburb of Mobile. It was pretty heady stuff for a seventeen-year-old.

2. A trip to Bear Creek, Alabama, to visit John T. Pike's family. We had driven all the way from Oxnard, California, and they "rolled out the red carpet" for us. John was one of 11 children, so there was no shortage of family. It was wonderful. So many people. They set up makeshift tables with planks on top of sawhorses and covered the boards over with whatever was available. My fifteen-year-old sister, Norma Jean, was with us. She bit into a banana sandwich, and her expression was priceless. Wish I had had a camera! The welcoming friendliness of everyone was awesome and something I will treasure forever. And we had so much fun encouraging one of the toddlers to try to pronounce "Tuscaloosa." It always came out "Tuscagoose."

All of us have come a long way since I first set foot in Alabama. But one thing has NOT changed. The warmth and friendliness of the Alabama people today is still the same.

I am happy to see that the Airbus' final assembly plant at Mobile's Brookley Aeroplex is just one more thing to rejoice over in Mobile, Alabama.

BEAR CREEK, ALABAMA

Bear Creek is a town located in Marion County (the northwestern portion of the state.) The population, according to the 2005 U.S. Census was estimated at about 1,021.

Trip to Bear Creek on May 23, 2013

David Hampton (our mentor and guide) led us up to Bear Creek early after he had dropped his children off at Holy Spirit High. Good thing – the two lane highways up there are not well-marked. Everyone seems to know their way around. And the locals tend to measure distance in minutes, not miles.

Not much is known about the early history of Bear Creek. The picture of the plaque on the brick wall of Bear Creek No. 1 Baptist Church shows that the church was organized in 1899.

The Bear Creek Cemetery, which is adjacent to the church, has headstones so old and weathered they aren't legible. But there are many newer headstones, and the cemetery is very well-kept.

Our first stop was the convenience store/gas station. The ladies on duty were very friendly. Our California license plates sparked a conversation. Seems everyone knew or was related to someone in California. It was like a step back in time. Lots of fun.

David Hampton and his uncle, John T. Pike, were both born in Bear Creek. I had promised John I would take pictures of his old home place and also his parents' headstones in the cemetery.

Bear Creek, Alabama. The Pike Family home place.

The old Pike home didn't look much different from when I had visited there in 1956 except a garage had been added onto the house. And David Hampton's old home place was still just down the street.

Bear Creek had escaped being struck by the tornado, but they had been very involved in coming to the aid of their neighboring towns of Phil Campbell (75% destroyed) and Hackleburg (totally destroyed.)

David Hampton led us over to Phil Campbell and introduced us to a couple who took refuge in a crawl space under their house. It saved their lives.

David had to head back to Tuscaloosa, so we bid him a fond farewell and were on our own the remainder of our time in Alabama.

PHIL CAMPBELL, ALABAMA

History

There is no shortage of history on the town of Phil Campbell. In the 1880s, a railroad work crew leader and engineer who was originally from England established a work camp near present-day Phil Campbell. The town was named after him and became the only town in Alabama to bear both the first and last names of an individual.

Phil Campbell is located in Franklin County in the northwest corner of the state. As of the 2000 census the population was 1,091.

Tornado

On April 27, 2011, Phil Campbell was about 75% destroyed by an EF5 tornado. About 30 people perished and the property loss was horrendous.

Trip to Phil Campbell on May 23, 2013

David Hampton led us from Bear Creek to Phil Campbell. There he introduced us to Pat and Philip Fleming who had survived the tornado. They and their little dog, Compass, had squeezed into a crawl space underneath their house, and they were unharmed. They are thankful to God for sparing their lives. They are devout Baptists and are going on a mission trip with their church to Ohio to help people there. They plan to rebuild their home.

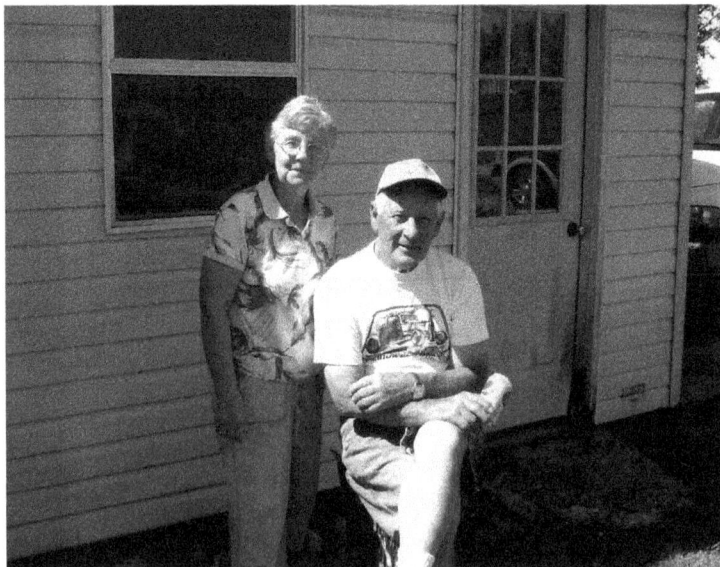

Pat and Philip Fleming survived the tornado in a crawl space underneath their house.

In the photo (right) our car is parked on a concrete slab that was their garage floor. The area in back of the car shows the devastation where houses once stood.

David Hampton directed us how to get to Hackleburg as he had to depart for Tuscaloosa.

HACKLEBURG, ALABAMA

Hackleburg is located in Marion County in the northwestern part of Alabama. The population as of the census of 2010 was 1,430. Its primary employer is the Wrangler Jeans plant.

History

Hackleburg first evolved in late Antebellum years along livestock drover routes from the Ohio Valley and Tennessee to South Alabama plantations. Its name was derived from the numerous hackle bushes that harmed the drovers' sheep.

The first stores did not appear until the 1905-08 time frame and the arrival of the Illinois Central Railroad. The number and variety of churches in the area indicates a strong faith-based community and family ties.

The People's Trust Bank, shown above, was destroyed by the EF5 Tornado which struck on April 27, 2011.

Tornado

On April 27, 2011, a devastating EF5 tornado struck Hackelburg, killing 29 people and destroying most of the town.

The Wrangler Distribution Center in Hackleburg was destroyed April 27, 2011, by the EF5 tornado.
Wrangler has since rebuilt the facility.

Trip to Hackleburg on May 23, 2013

The only evidence of a previous restaurant was boarded up, so we drove to the nearby town of Hamilton and had lunch at a very busy bar-b-que place. Food was good, and the people were friendly. The cashier spoke about how the destruction of Hackleburg had been a horrible blow to everyone.

One very bright note was that not only had the Wrangler Distribution Center been rebuilt in Hackleburg; they had continued to pay their employees and had transported them to a temporary facility while they rebuilt. Not one employee had lost his job or a paycheck due to the tornado!

MOBILE, ALABAMA

History

Known as the City of Six Flags, Mobile has been under the control of the French, English, Spanish, Sovereign Alabama, Confederate States of America, and the United States.

Mobile was founded in 1702 by Jean Beinville le Moyne and was named after the Manvilla Indians who had a settlement on the site.

A much-coveted port throughout its history, Mobile was particularly important to the Confederacy and is Alabama's only seaport. It is located 150 miles from New Orleans, 250 miles from Birmingham, and 350 miles from Atlanta.

Throughout its history, Mobile has endured many storms and hurricanes. In 1979 one of the most devastating hurricanes ever to hit the Central Gulf Coast was hurricane "Frederic." Frederic took an almost direct bearing on the historic city of Mobile. It struck during the night of September 12, 1979. Wind gusts of 145 miles per hour were recorded on the Dauphin Island Bridge. The bridge was so severely damaged that Dauphin Island was isolated until a new high rise span was built. Frederic was a Gulf Coast nightmare.

Other hurricanes have hit Mobile since Frederic but Mobile has not been their prime target. Hurricane Katrina on August 27, 2005, caused millions of dollars of damage to Mobile.

Severely damaged and isolated by Hurricane Frederic, the Dauphin Island Bridge awaits dismantling.

On Christmas Day in 2012, Mobile was hit by a tornado causing considerable property damage. No lives were lost.

The discovery of large natural gas deposits has brought drilling rigs into the Mobile Bay. The bay holds the second largest natural gas reserve in the world.

Among its strengths, Mobile has a deep-water port, a container terminal, two airports, five class-one railroads, and two major interstate highway systems. Mobile has been selected as the only site in the Western Hemisphere for assembling Airbus aircraft. Groundbreaking for this $600 million project at Mobile's Brookley Aeroplex was scheduled to take place in early 2013.

Mobile is on the west side of the Mobile River near the mouth of Mobile Bay. The city's river channel has been dredged over the years to accommodate oceangoing vessels of 40-foot draft.

Mobile was formerly a home for Carnival cruise ships. In early 2011 Carnival announced that despite fully booked cruises the company would cease operations from Mobile in October 2011. This cessation of cruise service left Mobile with an annual debt service of around $2 million related to the terminal.

On Valentine's Day 2013 the disabled Carnival cruise ship "Triumph" was towed by tugs into Mobile to offload passengers.

TUSCALOOSA, ALABAMA

History

Tuscaloosa was incorporated in 1819. Its name is derived from two Choctaw words, "Tuska," meaning warrior and the "Loosa" meaning black.

From its earliest days, Tuscaloosa was noted for its tree-lined avenues and its lovely old homes.

The Civil War wreaked havoc on Tuscaloosa. The Black Warrior River Bridge, the factories, and the principal buildings of the University of Alabama were left in ruins. The recovery and rebuilding after the Civil War was slow, but recover they did. Often called the "City of Oaks," the tree-lined avenues and beautiful homes are much in evidence today in the original old city. The University of Alabama is truly awesome.

Dinah Washington was born Ruth Lee Jones in Tuscaloosa in 1924. She would go on to become one of the all-time great jazz singers. She won a Grammy award in 1958 for "What a Difference a Day Makes."

The tornado which hit Tuscaloosa April 27, 2011, did a horrific amount of damage but it spared the University, the hospital, and the historic old downtown district.

The tornado struck a cruel blow but the city of Tuscaloosa is slowly making its way back. It appears to be rebuilding in a well-planned orderly manner; it is not just throwing up "quick fix" housing. They appear to be focusing on long term sustainable recovery. There is a lot of civic pride in Tuscaloosa, and it shows.

Trip To Tuscaloosa on May 19-23, 2013

This was my first trip to Tuscaloosa. The weather cooperated and was gorgeous the entire time we were there.

Our host and guide, David Hampton, and his 14-year-old son, Tristan came over to our motel to welcome and meet us upon our arrival. Toni, David's wife, and their 13-year-old daughter, Heather, had a social engagement that afternoon.

The Hampton family, of Tuscaloosa, AL. From left to right: David; his wife, Toni; daughter, Heather; author, Ollie Kirby; and son, Tristan Hampton.

We mapped out an orderly plan for touring the next day. Since David knew the city well, he picked us up in his vehicle after he dropped his children off at Holy Spirit Catholic High School.

The first part of our tour was the University of Alabama campus. It had not been hit by the tornado, thank God. Both my husband and I were totally unprepared for the magnificent beauty of the University. It was founded in 1831, many of the principal buildings had been destroyed in the Civil War, and today it is breathtaking. The enrollment was 33,602 in the fall of 2012. The University of Alabama is Tuscaloosa's largest employer.

Bryant-Denny Stadium is home to the University of Alabama *Crimson Tide* football team, one of the finest in the nation. The loyalty of their fans is legendary. The stadium has a seating capacity of 101,812. Sell-out crowds are the norm.

Next our host took us on a tour of the historic old downtown area which is in the midst of a public/private reinvestment, and we decided to explore this further on our own, which we did.

The last part of our guided tour for that day was the areas where the tornado had done its worst damage. It was heart-breaking. Tuscaloosa had 2,493 homes damaged, 1,612 homes severely damaged, and 1,257 homes destroyed. Two hundred forty-three commercial structures were damaged and 114 were destroyed. The debris and the rubble have been cleared away but the scars remain.

After David dropped us off for the day, my husband and I ventured back downtown where we first went to the Chamber of Commerce. Then we went to the *Which Wich* for lunch. It was packed with working folks on their lunch time. There we talked with two firefighters, Ron Cameron and Jason Jackson, who had experienced the tornado big time!

Jason Jackson was first on the scene. The Salvation Army facility was destroyed. The Red Cross facility was destroyed. The Emergency Relocation Center was destroyed. So it was volunteers who poured in and helped the police and firefighters. The Police Department and the Fire Department were so grateful for the army of volunteers who pitched right in. Those first responders worked through shifts to the point of exhaustion. It was heartbreaking work digging people out of the rubble. For a time, all of our modern technology was useless. The Communication Center had been knocked out. Cell phones didn't work. Power lines were down.

Our second day of touring Tuscaloosa was at a slower pace. We looked at some of the commercial space that had been damaged. *Full Moon Bar-B-Que* had been destroyed, but no lives were lost; the employees had taken refuge in a walk-in cold storage locker. The restaurant has rebuilt and expanded across the street from its former location. When we were there, the restaurant had been very busy.

Dillards department store was hit by the tornado. This was their second time of being struck and they elected to not rebuild.

Belks department store sustained damage to one corner of their building but they are doing fine. It was busy when I was in there.

All of us deserved some "fun time," so in the evening we went to a beautiful restaurant called Cypress Inn overlooking the Black Warrior River. It was excellent. Then we went to the Hamptons home for dessert and coffee. Turned on the news and watched in horror the broadcast on the Moore, Oklahoma, tornado. The kids were shocked that school children had not been sent home.

Wednesday, May 22nd, was our last full day in Tuscaloosa. David had made an appointment for me to meet with Mayor Walt Maddox at 1:00 p.m. My first thought when we were introduced was "He's too young and too good-looking to be the Mayor of Tuscaloosa!" What a heavy responsibility to carry.

After just a few minutes of talking with him, my thinking changed entirely. I found him to be extremely quick-witted and knowledgeable. He was such an interesting and personable individual that I almost forgot to ask him the questions I had jotted down, which were:

Question: Have you been successful in obtaining any government grants for rebuilding?
Answer: $64M in direct rebuilding; $5-25M more anticipated.

Question: Have you been able to attract any new businesses or companies?
Answer: Mercedes-Benz, our second largest employer, will be expanding its facility and its workforce by about 500 people. (At this point he asked David if he had taken me by the Mercedes-Benz plant. David replied that he had not but that he would.)

Question: What about the Army Reserve Training Center – will it be rebuilt?
Answer: The ARTC had already moved to Highway 61 south of Tuscaloosa before the tornado.

Question: What incentives are there for businesses to locate in Tuscaloosa?
Answer: Low property taxes. Return on their investment. Work ethic of our people.

My 30 minutes were up and Mayor Maddox had people waiting to see him. I came away from this meeting with profound respect for him, both as an individual and as a mayor.

After leaving the mayor's office David Hampton drove me down to see the huge Mercedes-Benz assembly plant south of town. It is a gated secure area so we couldn't enter but we could look down from one of the higher elevations on the highway and get a feeling of the vast size of the facility. It is Tuscaloosa's second largest employer, exceeded only by the University of Alabama.

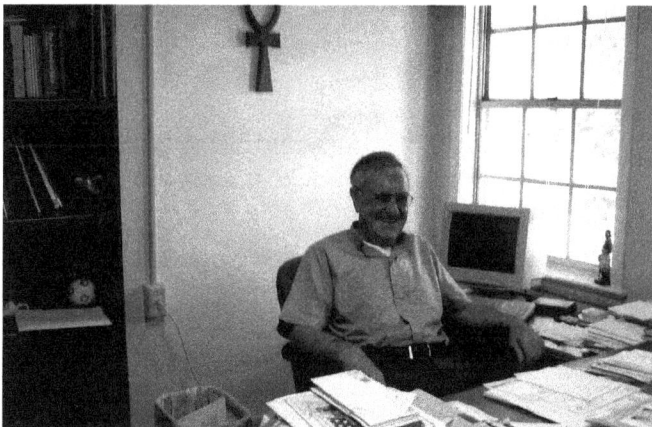

Father Deasy, the parish priest at Holy Spirit Catholic Church, Tuscaloosa, Alabama.

Our next appointment was at 3:00 p.m. with Father Deasy at Holy Spirit Catholic Church. Father Deasy is Irish, goes back to Ireland for a month every year, and has an endearing Irish brogue. When I mentioned that my maternal grandmother had been Irish and her name was Sullivan he said, "We have lots of Soo-le-vans in my part of Ireland.

Photo by Tristan Hampton
Holy Spirit Catholic Church, Tuscaloosa, Alabama

Father Deasy was in Tuscaloosa at the time of the tornado. His church turned their Parish Hall into a shelter for the Hispanics. Many of them spoke very little English and were afraid to go to the other shelters. Those who were bilingual acted as interpreters and everyone helped one another. Just a short distance away, the tornado had leveled everything. Thank God it left this wonderful church untouched.

Father Deasy explained that the Catholic Church for centuries has been known as a place of refuge, a "safe haven."

In the evening after dinner at the Hampton home I had the privilege of an interview with Thomas Furlough, another dinner guest. He is a music teacher at both Tuscaloosa Magnet and Eastwood Middle Schools. He teaches orchestra. He is also in the National Guard.

The Alberta Elementary School was totally demolished by the tornado. The Acting Superintendent had

Holy Spirit Catholic High School, Tuscaloosa, Alabama

closed the school, so there was no one in the building.

Tom said they set up an emergency center in Leland Lanes Bowling Center and worked out of there, dispensing supplies, etc.

Time constraints precluded us viewing the Tuscaloosa Amphitheater. It is located in downtown Tuscaloosa on the banks of the Black Warrior River. It seats 7,470 people.

**Tristan Hampton, and his sister, Heather, both students at
Holy Spirit Catholic High School**

Summary

Without the considerable help and hard work of David Hampton and his family, this beautiful chapter on Tuscaloosa would not have been possible. He was my mentor and my guide.

Although David was not born in Tuscaloosa (he was born in Bear Creek, Alabama), he has lived there for many years and knows the city well. In advance of my arrival, he had set up interviews and paved the way for maximum utilization of my time. What a blessing.

David's wife Toni; his son, Tristan; and his daughter, Heather; showed my husband and me what "Southern Hospitality" really means. They welcomed us into their home to "break bread together." We had never met before, and we are now friends for life.

CHAPTER TWO

ARIZONA

History

Native Americans were the first Arizonians and are still a major influence throughout the state. The Mexican influence is strong as well.

Phoenix was finally chosen as the territorial capitol in 1889. Then in 1912 Arizona was the last of the contiguous 48 states to be admitted to the union.

Four Corners Monument

The Four Corners Monument near Window Rock, Arizona is the only place in the country where four states meet - Arizona, Utah, Colorado and New Mexico.

Grand Canyon National Park

The Grand Canyon National Park in northwestern Arizona defies description. Millions of people from all over the world visit it every year.

Although most people think of Arizona as being desert, mountains and plateaus comprise more than half of the land.

Mining in Arizona

Copper mining built Arizona, and Morenci Copper Mine is the largest copper mine in North America. It is also one of the largest in the world. The town of Morenci is just south of the mine and an old aerial photo circa 1910 is included herein. It was a company-owned town built by Phelps Dodge. Morenci is part of the Safford Micropolitan Statistical Area, and had a population of 1,879 at the 2000 Census.

Pictures of the Morenci Mine weren't readily available so I dug through an old photo album and came up with a couple of aerial shots which my husband took from the co-pilot seat of a Cessna 182 in 1974. We had flown down to Safford to see Bob and Madelaine Becker. Bob was an engineer for Stearns Roger, working on a copper concentration and leach plant for Phelps Dodge at Morenci Mine.

Bob wanted to view his job site from the air, and it was a beautiful day so away we went. Since Bob had been a helicopter pilot in Vietnam, he certainly had no fear of flying - even with a female at the controls! Copper mining was booming at that time. Life was good. None of us had an inkling of the hardship that lay ahead for Morenci.

Copper Mine Strike of 1983

The recession of 1981 had a disastrous effect on the copper industry. The price of copper plummeted by almost 50%. Massive layoffs occurred statewide.

Morenci Copper Mine, located in Morenci, Arizona, is the largest copper mining operation in North America and one of the largest copper mines in the world.

Since Morenci Copper Mine is the largest in North America, it took a big hit. People were hungry. People were angry. And Phelps Dodge (the owner) was hemorrhaging red ink. The unions and Phelps Dodge could not come to an agreement. It was an explosive situation.

July 30, 1983, a strike began. Thousands of workers walked out, and violence erupted. It was an ugly time in labor/management relations. Negotiations continued to fail between the unions and Phelps Dodge. A federal mediator was called in for negotiations between the two sides.

In September 1984, all the workers voted on whether or not they wanted the unions. Almost unanimously the workers voted out the unions. The unions appealed to the National Labor Relations Board in an attempt to halt decertification.

Finally the strike ended on February 19, 1986, when the National Labor Relations Board rejected the union's appeals. It was over.

Phelps Dodge restructured and avoided bankruptcy. World copper prices began to make a comeback. Then in 2007, Morenci Copper Mine was acquired by Freeport-McMoRan. It is still in business today.

Yarnell, AZ, - 2013 Wildfire - Granite Mountain Hotshots

On June 30, 2013, nineteen firefighters of the elite team known as the Granite Mountain Hotshots died while fighting the Yarnell wildfire. Prescott's Fire Station 7 was the home of the Hotshots.

The 19 firefighters were:

Eric Marsh (Arizona)
Travis Turbyfill (Arizona)
Wade Parker (Arizona)
Andrew Ashcraft (Arizona)
Clayton Whitted (Arizona)
William Warneke (Arizona)
Joe Thurston (Utah)
Christopher MacKenzie (California)
Anthony Rose (Illinois)
John Percin (Oregon)
Grant McKee (Arizona)
Jesse Steed (Arizona)
Robert Caldwell (Arizona)
Garret Zuppiger (Arizona)
Sean Misner (California)
Scott Norris (Arizona)
Dustin Deford (Montana)
Travis Carter (Arizona)
Kevin Woyjeck (California)

Yarnell Hill Fire, where 19 members of the elite team known as the Granite Mountain Hotshots lost their lives.

One Hotshot team member, Brendan McDonough, age 21, was the lone survivor. He served as the team's lookout and was in the process of moving his truck to safer ground when his fellow Hotshots were overcome by the fire.

Darrell Willis, division chief of the Prescott Fire Department and the "father" of Granite Mountain Hotshots, had a personal relationship with each of the firefighters.

The Granite Mountain Hot Shots, 2013

At the July 9, 2013, memorial ceremony in Prescott, an estimated 1,000 firefighters from all 50 states, Canada, and other countries came to pay tribute to the 19 firefighters who perished in the wildfire. Fire Chief Dan Fraijo spoke of the bond between the firefighters. There is always the threat that something could go wrong, the threat that they could be injured or, God forbid, be killed in the line of duty.

Yarnell, Arizona, wildfire, June 2013, where nineteen firefighters of the elite team known as the Granite Mountain Hotshots died while fighting the fire.

A task force was formed by the Arizona State Forestry Division to investigate the firefighter's deaths. The fire was caused by a lightning strike on June 28, 2013. The extreme drought, chaparral and dry grass provided ample fuel for the raging fire.

According to the Professional Fire Fighters of Arizona, three official fundraising efforts to help the families of the victims were undertaken immediately. Other local fundraising events were quickly organized as well.

Friends, neighbors, churches and charitable organizations were the mainstay of emotional support after this terrible loss.

CHAPTER THREE

ARKANSAS

History

Exploration of the region which is now Arkansas began with Hernando de Soto in 1541. In 1686 Henri de Tonti established the Mississippi Valley's first European settlement. The eastern boundary of present-day Arkansas is the Mississippi River. Spain gained control of the area in 1763 but returned it to France 37 years later.

The United States acquired the region in 1803 as part of the Louisiana Purchase, and in 1836 Arkansas entered the Union as a slave-holding state.

Historic Places of Current Interest

Crater of Diamonds State Park near Murfreesboro in Pike County is claimed to be the only diamond-producing site in the world open to the public.

In 1962, Sam Walton opened the first Walmart store in Rogers, Arkansas. Walmart, the largest retailer in the world, is headquartered in Bentonville which is a picturesque Ozark town in the northwest corner of the state.

Bentonville also is home to Crystal Bridges Museum of American Art. The galleries include such treasures as Asher B. Durand's *Kindred Spirits*, Maxine Parrish's *The Lantern Bearers*, Norman Rockwell's *Rosie the Riveter* and Andy Warhol's *Dolly Parton.*

On Friday, May 24, 2013, we had a chance to go through Crystal Bridges Museum. The traveling art exhibit of Norman Rockwell was there, and I was fortunate to be able to get a ticket to see it (someone had been unable to use their ticket). What a joy that was. The place was packed! Admission to the museum itself is free, but tickets have to be purchased in advance for the traveling exhibits. Thanks to the generosity of Alice Walton, more Americans now have the opportunity to enjoy great art.

Hot Springs National Park in western Arkansas is quite different from the other national parks. Portions of it are nearly surrounded by the city of Hot Springs. In 1832 (nearly 100 years before it became a national park) the federal government set aside the springs and surrounding area as the country's first park-type federal reservation.

Ice Storm of 2009

In early 2009 all across the northern part of Arkansas was hit by a deadly ice storm. This storm extended into Indiana, Ohio, Kentucky, Oklahoma and Missouri. Kentucky was the hardest hit. It was Kentucky's worst natural disaster.

In northern Arkansas 119,000 were without power, some for as long as a week. Modern technology in many areas was totally useless. Those who were fortunate enough to have back-up generators helped those who did not. But in isolated areas they were on their own.

photo courtesy of U.S. Army

Arkansas Ice Storm in 2009

"Old-timers" were often best equipped to cope. Wood-burning fireplaces were a blessing. They brought out the old manually-operated can openers and heated food in the fireplace. If the water coming out of the faucet (if it would come out at all) was "murky," they'd step outside VERY carefully and get some ice to melt! Didn't hear of anybody getting poisoned from melting ice.

Many of the deaths from the ice storm were from carbon monoxide poisoning or hypothermia.

Roads were not only ice-coated, but they were often impassable due to downed power lines or trees.

CABOT, ARKANSAS

Interesting Trivia - County Line Changes

Cabot is in northern Lonoke County. In 1860 that area was in Prairie County. In 1870 it was in Pulaski County. By 1880 it was in Lonoke County. A person could have lived in three different counties between 1860 and 1880 and never moved!

Tornadoes of March 29, 1976

On March 29, 1976, the town of Cabot, Arkansas, was ripped apart by several EF3-EF4 tornadoes. The strongest one went through the downtown area killing five people, injuring others and causing millions of dollars' worth of damage to businesses, homes and property.

Lucinda "Cindy" (Johnson) Ransick was a senior in high school at Russellville, Arkansas, when the tornadoes occurred. She was old enough to go over to Cabot and work with a group of people helping clean up and start to rebuild. People from neighboring towns, church groups, etc., all rolled up their sleeves and pitched in.

Mayflower, Arkansas, Tornado of April 27, 2014

On April 27, 2014, a massive tornado literally flattened the small town of Mayflower, Arkansas. At least 16 people were killed, and property damage was extensive. The tornado was so powerful that semi-trucks were lifted off Interstate 40 like toys. Mayflower is located just north of Little Rock, Arkansas.

RUSSELLVILLE, ARKANSAS

History

Russellville is the county seat and largest city in Pope County. It is home to Arkansas Tech University (formerly Arkansas Polytechnic College.)

Arkansas Nuclear One, the state's only nuclear power plant, is located at Russellville.

Russellville borders beautiful Lake Dardanelle as well as the Arkansas River. This results in its hosting many sporting events and fishing tournaments.

The first settler in the area was P.C. Holledger in 1834. A year later, Dr. Thomas Russell bought Holledger's house. The first business to be established in the town was owned by a Mr. Shinn. When the town's residents decided to name the town the choices were Shinnville or Russellville. Russellville won. The town was incorporated on June 7, 1870.

The building of Interstate 40 in 1956 was a boon to Russellville's growth, much like the railroad was in the 1870s. And a major economic boost came as a result of the completion of a dam near the Arkansas River crossing between Dardanelle and Russellville in 1965. The dam created a lake, which led to the establishment of Lake Dardanelle State Park.

Russellville's population has shown a steady growth from 5,900 in 1940 to 27,920 in 2010. It has a diverse manufacturing base. Russellville is home to divisions of such corporations as Tyson Foods, Inc., etc. Forty-eight manufacturing plants employ more than 8,300 people

Russellville provides modern amenities but it has retained its small town friendliness and charm.

Lucinda "Cindy" (Johnson) Ransick

On January 28, 2013, I interviewed "Cindy" who was born and raised in Russellville. Her mother, Barbara (Mills) Johnson was born in Paris, Arkansas. Her father, Marvin Johnson, was born in Ft. Smith, Arkansas. They met at college (Arkansas Polytechnic College which is now ATU.)

As a child Cindy remembers how she and her parents would go down in the basement and get under the pool table whenever a tornado warning sounded. Her father said with the pool table's heavy slate bed that was the safest place to be.

On March 29, 1976, when the town of Cabot, Arkansas, was ripped apart by tornadoes, Cindy, who was a senior at Russellville High School went with a group of people to Cabot to help with clean-up and rebuilding.

Cindy must have inherited many traits from her mother who was a school teacher with a big heart. Whenever a disaster happened in Russellville, her mother would say, "Let's put up a tent in the yard and feed these people."

Barbara "Bobbi" (Beasley) Granville

An interesting bit of Russellville history came from Bobbi Granville. She was born May 30, 1938, upon Norristown Mountain south of Russellville. Bobbi was an only child. When she was three years old, World War II broke out and her father went into the U.S. Navy. Her mother went to Los Angeles and got a job in an aircraft plant as a "Rosie the Riveter." Bobbi was left with her aunt and uncle upon Norristown Mountain. They had no children of their own, but there was no lack of cousins, etc., for companionship for Bobbi.

Her aunt, Illah (Parrish) McAnulty, was the local school teacher. The schoolhouse where she taught was a rock structure. It was one long room and a curtain was strung across the center to separate it into two sections. Elementary school was conducted in one section and high school was conducted in the other part.

Their house was up on top of the mountain, and the school was quite a distance down the unpaved road so her uncle would drive them to school. Bobbi remembers one winter day he hooked up the sleigh and took them to school. In the springtime he would take them in the buggy.

Mountain Springs School, Russellville, Arkansas, circa 1925.

Included here is a picture of the old original school up on Norristown Mountain. The picture is circa 1925. Six of Bobbi's aunts and uncles are in the picture. It was a very large school with a big attendance. It was an old wooden frame structure. The rock schoolhouse which Bobbi attended was later converted into Russellville Fire Station No. 2. That building was later expanded to accommodate two fire truck bays.

Conditions were primitive up on the mountain: no electricity, no indoor plumbing. But Bobbi has wonderful memories of those few early childhood years spent up on Norristown Mountain outside Russellville. Her maternal grandparents were James Parrish and Katherine (Moore) Parrish. Her paternal grandparents were Evan and Elizabeth Beasley.

Present Day Russellville

My husband and I took a trip to Russellville on Friday, May 24, 2013. We ate breakfast at the *Old South* restaurant which was your typical Midwestern café. It was busy with what appeared to be a mixture of business people and retirees. I asked one of the gentlemen sitting at the table near our booth if the historic old Shinn Building was still in existence. His name was Mr. Carnahan. He said it was, and that half of it was occupied by a very nice Italian restaurant and the other half was some sort of specialty store. He even told us how to find it so we could take pictures. The half shown in the photograph which has a red and white striped awning is the Italian restaurant.

The Shinn Building, built in 1875.

Present day Russellville seems to have a healthy economy. Graduations were over at the local college and one elderly gentleman was complaining that God only knew when he would see his granddaughter again as she had gone off to some big city to seek her fame and fortune!

VILONIA, ARKANSAS

Vilonia is a small town north of Little Rock, Arkansas.

At 7:30 p.m. on April 25, 2011, a tornado struck the small community of Vilonia and claimed the lives of four people. This was part of the massive outbreak that killed 253 people in Alabama.

In addition to killing four people, many more were injured. Numerous structures were damaged or destroyed. Within five minutes, local firefighters began search and rescue efforts. Eighty-five members of the National Guard were deployed to Vilonia.

One of the things especially hard hit was the utilities. Overhead power poles were snapped like toothpicks.

All of the area churches immediately banded together to help in the recovery effort. Their love and compassion to those in need was awesome.

As if the horrible tornado of April 25, 2011, wasn't enough tragedy, on April 28, 2014, Vilonia, Arkansas was hit by another massive tornado which practically flattened the town. It was the same tornado that struck Mayflower.

CHAPTER FOUR

COLORADO

History

In 1540 Francisco de Coronado led an expedition through what is now southeastern Colorado. It wasn't until 1803 that the United States acquired the area as part of the Louisiana Purchase.

When gold was discovered at what is now Arvada, Colorado, and then other gold strikes in 1858, Colorado's gold rush began. Prospectors, saloons, brothels and lawlessness abounded for some time.

Colorado became the 38th state in the Union on August 1, 1876.   And in 1881 the Ute tribes were forced into reservations.

In 1906 the U.S. Mint at Denver issued its first coins. They still give guided tours but for security reasons they do not have a set schedule. And they don't give out any samples.

Colorado's first commercial ski resort opened for business in 1947 in Aspen.

The United States Air Force Academy was established in 1954 in Colorado Springs. Its majestic Cadet Chapel at 6,008 feet above sea level is something to behold.

But if you really want to "get high" take a trip up to the top of Pike's Peak, at 14,110 feet above sea level. The view from the top inspired Katherine Lee Bates to write *America the Beautiful* in 1893.

Race car drivers and "wanna be" racers love the winding road to the top of Pike's Peak. That's not for me. The next time I go, it will be via the cog railway out of Manitou Springs! And I will be wearing a warm coat. The temperature at the base of the mountain is about 30 degrees warmer than the summit. And surprisingly enough, Zebulon Pike, after whom it was named, never made it to the summit.

Starkville Mine Explosion of 1910

On October 8, 1910, a coal dust explosion at the Starkville Mine near Trinidad, Colorado, killed 56 men. The Denver Post, in a blog post August 24, 2012, described the explosion as follows: "A spark from a short circuit on an overhead trolley line ignited coal dust, causing an explosion which was heard and felt in Trinidad seven miles away.

"Huge rocks and timbers were blown hundreds of feet from the mouth of the mine and 40 feet of tunnel collapsed, closing the entrance.

"Rescuers from miles around worked in relays to reach the buried miners. It wasn't until three days after the explosion that the first bodies were reached. There were no survivors.

"Inspection determined that the mine had been insufficiently sprinkled to keep the coal dust damp, though repeatedly warned by the state.

Almeron Newman File Photo

Starkville Mine Explosion of 1910. Group of rescuers awaiting orders at new mine entrance

"On December 1, 1910, a jury found the Colorado Fuel & Iron Company guilty of gross negligence resulting in the death of the 56 miners." ("1910 Explosion at Starkville Mine in Colorado Killed 56." The Archive Web. The Denver Post, 24 Aug. 2012. Web. 28 May 2014.)

BIG THOMPSON CANYON, COLORADO

Big Thompson Flood, July 31, 1976

The Big Thompson Flood was the deadliest flash flood in Colorado's recorded history. And it occurred at the height of the tourist season.

Record-breaking rain came down. A 20-foot wall of water crashed down through the V-shaped canyon taking everything in its path with it. This monstrous flood killed 144 people and injured 150. It took out Highway 34, the only road down the canyon.

COLORADO SPRINGS, COLORADO

Black Forest Fire, June 11-20, 2013

This was Colorado's worst ever forest fire. It burned 16,000 acres in nine days and killed two people. More than 500 structures were destroyed.

More than 400 firefighters battled this ferocious fire. Colorado National Guard sent 140 people to assist. They managed to keep the fire outside the city limits of Colorado Springs, Colorado's second largest city.

Photo by Helen H. Richardson/The Denver Post

A house is fully engulfed with flames in the midst of the Black Forest Fire northeast of Colorado Springs on June 12, 2013.

It is unknown how the blaze started.
Two straight years of drought in the state makes the forest very vulnerable to fires.

DENVER, COLORADO

Denver Flood of June 16, 1965 (South Platte River)

Residences and houses along Santa Fe Drive in Denver were evacuated. The amount of damage was eventually set at around $540 million in the Denver area and people lost their lives. The flood of the South Platte River knocked out every bridge from Bowles Avenue to Colfax Avenue.

I will never forget that flood. I was living in Lakewood (a suburb of Denver) and was getting married in Boulder on June 20, 1965. A few days before the wedding we had a difficult time getting into Denver to pick up our wedding bands. I think we paid all of $65 for both rings and we still wear them today!

Glenwood Springs, Colorado, South Canyon Fire Disaster – July 6, 1994

On the afternoon of July 6, 1994, one of the worst fire disasters in Colorado history occurred.

Lightning sparked a fire on July 2, 1994, about seven miles west of Glenwood Springs. It was small and away from private property so it was assigned a low priority.

By July 4th even though the fire had only burned about three acres, nearby residents were getting very concerned, prompting authorities to take action. It was decided to commence the rugged uphill fight the following morning.

Courtesy of http://wildlandfireleadership.blogspot.com

Storm King Mountain during the South Canyon fire, near Glenwood Springs, Colorado.

Firefighters began their uphill march from the west on July 5th and began constructing fire lines to control the blaze. Smokejumpers joined the fight against the fire. Everyone worked well into the night but quit because of danger of falling rocks.

On July 6th twenty Hotshots from Prineville, Oregon, were rushed in to aid in the battle. In the afternoon a dry cold front swept into that area, increasing the winds and fire activity. By 4 P.M. the fire had jumped the fire line below the firefighters and was racing up the steep densely vegetated terrain towards the firefighters. They were trapped and couldn't outrun the fire.

Twelve firefighters perished. Two helitack firefighters tried to flee to the northwest, and they also died.

The twelve firefighters who died that day were all from the elite Prineville, Oregon, Hotshots. The two helitack firefighters who died were from Grand Junction, Colorado.

The following firefighters lost their lives on July 6, 1994:

PRINEVILLE, OREGON, HOTSHOTS

Beck, Kathi, Eugene, Oregon
Bickett, Tamera, Powell Butte, Oregon
Blecha, Scott, Clatskanie, Oregon
Brinkley, Levi, Burns, Oregon
Dunbar, Doug, Redmond, Oregon
Holtby, Bonnie, Prineville, Oregon
Johnson, Rob, Redmond, Oregon
Hagen, Terri, Prineville, Oregon
Kelso, John, Prineville, Oregon
Mackey, Don, Hamilton, Montana (Missoula Smokejumper)
Roth, Roger, McCall, Idaho (McCall Smokejumper)
Thrash, James, McCall, Idaho (McCall Smokejumper)

HELITACK CREWMEMBERS

Browning, Robert, Grand Junction, Colorado
Tyler, Richard, Grand Junction, Colorado

WELD COUNTY, COLORADO

On July 8, 2013, a farmer near Brighton, Colorado, used his John Deere tractor and a tiller to plow a fire break across a hayfield to prevent a fire from spreading.

Lightning had started the fire, and it had quickly consumed 20-30 acres of an 80-acre hayfield. Eric Howard got in his tractor and dug a firebreak close to the flames to try to halt the fire's progress.

Eric Howard's quick action held the fire in check until firefighters were able to extinguish it. What a brave man!

Eric Howard plowing firebreak, Weld County Fire, Colorado, July 8, 2013.

WINDSOR, COLORADO

EF3 Tornado of May 22, 2008

On May 22, 2008, the small town of Windsor, Colorado, was hit by a mile-wide tornado around lunch time. One resident in a trailer at a campground was killed. Dozens of houses and dozens of vehicles were badly damaged. Several semis were rolled off U.S. 85 north of Greeley.

Larry and Jan Confer, of Windsor, Colorado.

I interviewed one couple who had experienced the tornado first-hand, Larry and Jan Confer. Larry was at work at Ace Hardware in Windsor when the tornado hit. All of the employees moved to the sturdiest place in the building (away from the windows) until the storm passed. Nobody was injured. Vehicles in the parking lot, including Larry's, were damaged.

Jan Confer was at work in the J.C. Penney's store in Greeley, Colorado, when the tornado struck. Employees followed safety procedures. There were no injuries.

CHAPTER FIVE

GEORGIA

History

In 1540, Hernando de Soto, his soldiers and his priests explored what is now the southeastern United States. Savannah was a key seaport even before the Revolutionary War. Georgia was founded as England's 13th and last colony in 1733.

In 1837 an army engineer surveyed routes for the Western and Atlantic Railroad that would provide a trade route west, and the city of Atlanta was born.

In 1838 the Cherokee Indians were forced to leave their tribal lands and relocate to Territorial Oklahoma via the "Trail of Tears."

The Civil War began in 1861. In 1863, General Sherman's Union troops looted and burned Atlanta on their "March to the Sea."

Andersonville Prison

Opened in 1864 in southwestern Georgia (Macon County), Andersonville Prison was a stockade where captured Union soldiers were imprisoned. It was described as a "Hell on Earth." Built to house 10,000 prisoners, Andersonville at one time confined more than 32,000. The impoverished Confederate government was unable to provide even the bare necessities of life. The mortality rate was enormous.

Natural Disasters – Tornadoes

Adairsville, Georgia EF-3 Tornado

On Wednesday, January 30, 2013, a tornado packing 160 miles per hour winds tore through Adairsville, population 4,648 causing two deaths and huge property damage. This is "Bible Belt" country and the local Church of God immediately began registering volunteers. More than 461 volunteers signed up.

Ringgold EF-4 Tornado, April 27, 2011

Ringgold, population 3,580, was a part of the path of tornadoes that ripped through five states on its deadly path all the way from the Deep South to Canada April 25-28, 2011. Eight people died in Ringgold which is in Catoosa County. In Catoosa County itself there were 20 deaths.

Interesting history in Ringgold. It is close to the Tennessee state line and is in what is known as the "Bible Belt." At one time they put up a public display of the Ten Commandments but, after complaints, took it down.

Ringgold capitalizes on its close proximity to the Tennessee border. Dolly Parton, who lived in Tennessee, wanted to get married but thought it might harm her professional career. So she drove across the line to Ringgold, Georgia, and secretly "tied the knot."

Gainesville, Georgia – April 6, 1936

The worst tornado in Georgia history occurred in Gainesville on April 6, 1936. 203 lives were lost and more than 1600 people were injured. Two different tornadoes from different directions collided in downtown Gainesville at 8:27 AM on April 6, 1936. The Catholic Church was miraculously spared when the tornadoes veered around it.

The Cooper Pants Factory, a multi-story building, collapsed, killing about 70 workers. A downtown department store where school children had taken refuge collapsed killing them all.

The population at that time was around 10,000. Today's population is around 33,800.

Offices along South Main Street in Gainesville following three tornadoes that touched down in the early morning of April 6, 1936.

Tornado of June 1, 1903, in Gainesville

Gainesville was struck by a deadly tornado on June 1, 1903, which killed 100 people.

Hurricanes and Tropical Storms

Tropical Storm Alberto – July 4, 1994

South of Atlanta Airport, *Alberto* dumped 25 inches of rain in less than 24 hours. Thirty-four people were killed, more than 50,000 were displaced from their homes, and at least 400 coffins were forced from water-logged graves into flooded streets.

Hurricane Katrina, 2005

Western Georgia took a hit from Hurricane Katrina on August 29, 2005. Georgia became the destination for more than 100,000 evacuees from the Gulf States which strained the resources of Georgia.

Wildfires in Georgia

On April 16, 2007, a downed power line ignited drought-parched forest floors. Nearly 564,000 acres were burned in Georgia and Florida. More than 3,300 firefighters from 44 states, Canada and Puerto Rico came to battle the fire.

CHAPTER SIX

IDAHO

History

Idaho is a mountainous state located in the northwestern region of the United States. It was admitted to the Union on July 3, 1890, as the 43rd state.

Idaho's nickname is the "Gem State" because nearly every known type of gemstone has been found there. It is also sometimes called the "Potato State" because of its bountiful and popular crop of potatoes. It produces more potatoes than any other state in the nation.

Tourism is a mainstay of Idaho's economy. Beautiful lakes, rivers and waterfalls abound. Carved by the Snake River, Hell's Canyon is North America's deepest river gorge with a width of 10 miles and a depth of 7,913 feet below He Devil Peak in the Seven Devils Mountains.

Idaho's State Capitol, constructed between 1905 and 1920, is the only capitol building in the nation to be heated by geothermal water from a source 3,000 feet below the ground.

A 13-foot-tall metal sculpture of a miner at Kellogg, Idaho, memorializes the Sunshine Mine disaster of May 2, 1972. The statue stands behind 91 miniature tombstones, one for each miner who perished in the fire at America's largest silver mine.

The state seal of Idaho is the only state seal in the United States designed by a woman (Emma Edwards Green).

The Decline of the Mining Industry

An area in the Idaho panhandle (Northern Idaho) once was a booming mining district. No more, and it is doubtful if it will ever rebound. The small towns in Silver Valley are dying. They have been withering away for 20 years.

The mines of Silver Valley east of Couer d'Alene Lake were once the richest silver producers in the world. In 1981 thousands of miners lost their jobs when the sinking price of silver forced the mines to close. Then in 1983 the Environmental Protection Agency (EPA) declared the area a federal Superfund site. The stigma of pollution still persists.

Sunshine Mine (about 8 miles east of Kellogg, Idaho) Disaster

On May 2, 1972, one hundred seventy-three men began work at 7:00 a.m. at the Sunshine Mine. The mine produced silver, copper and antimony. Ninety-one men died of carbon monoxide poisoning leaving 91 families behind.

At 5:43 p.m. May 9th they found two miners, Tom Wilkinson and Ron Flory alive and in good condition at a diamond drill station 1,800 feet west of the No. 10 shaft. They were taken to the No. 12 borehole and hoisted out of the mine. They were the last survivors found.

Miners Tom Wilkinson and Ron Flory were the last two survivors found in the mine.

CHAPTER SEVEN

INDIANA

History

The French were the first Europeans to explore the region. Robert Cavalier and Sieur de la Salle traveled up the St. Joseph River in 1679-1680 to Indiana.

At the conclusion of the French and Indian War the area was claimed by Britain. After the British defeat in the American Revolutionary War, the entire trans-Allegheny region was ceded to the United States in 1783.

In 1816, Indiana became the 19th state to be admitted to the Union. Then in 1842 the University of Notre Dame was founded at South Bend. Indiana's Capitol and largest city is Indianapolis.

Located in the Midwestern United States, Indiana is one of the eight states which make up the Great Lakes region, with its 41 miles of shoreline on Lake Michigan. The Port of Indiana operates the state's largest shipping port. This area is the industrial hub of Indiana.

Indiana is a leader in agriculture, with corn its principal crop. Much of the limestone used in the United States is quarried in Indiana. Indiana limestone was used in the construction of the Empire State Building in New York City, the Pentagon and National Cathedral in Washington, D.C., as well as several state capitols.

The Indianapolis Motor Speedway hosted the first *Indy 500* race on May 30th, 1911, two years after it opened. Equipped to seat an audience of more than 250,000, the Speedway is the world's largest sporting arena.

Santa Claus, Indiana receives hundreds of thousands of letters addressed to *Santa* every year, each of which is responded to individually.

EVANSVILLE, INDIANA

History

The city was founded by Hugh McGary in 1812 and incorporated in 1819. It is the commercial, medical and cultural hub of Southwestern Indiana and the Illinois-Indiana-Kentucky tri-state area. It is the third-largest city in Indiana. Evansville had a population of 117,429 as of the 2010 census.

Evansville is situated on a horseshoe bend in the beautiful Ohio River. Its location has been an important factor in its broad economic base in the region. The building of the Wabash and Erie Canal, which connected the Great Lakes to the Ohio River greatly accelerated Evansville's growth. The canal was completed in 1853. In that same year, Evansville's first railroad was opened to Terre Haute.

The first highway bridge to cross the Ohio River and connect Evansville with Henderson, Kentucky was built in 1932. At one time Evansville was the center of fine furniture factories. They also built paddlewheels for steamboats. Now only one remains, Karges, which still makes the finest furniture produced in the United States.

World War II

During WWII, Evansville was the largest inland producer of LSTs (Tank Landing Ships). The inland location was very important as German spies looked more for coastal locations. Evansville also produced a specific version of the P-47 Thunderbolt. Evansville produced a total of 6,242 P-47s, almost half of the P-47s made during the war, and 167 LSTs.

Port Facilities, Evansville, Indiana

The location of Evansville on the banks of the beautiful Ohio River has been key to so many benefits. The fact that it has been a U.S. Customs Port of Entry for over 125 years was a pretty well-kept secret during World War II. The enemy was looking for coastal ports of entry, not someplace in the Heartland of the United States.

Since Evansville is a U.S. Customs Port of Entry, international cargo can be shipped in bond directly to Evansville. No wonder major barge lines are a common sight on the Ohio River since Evansville connects with all central U.S. river markets and the Great Lakes. Evansville also connects with international markets via New Orleans.

In spite of its size, Evansville has retained that Midwest friendliness and charm. The *Tropicana Evansville* (formerly *Casino Aztar)* on the Ohio River was the first riverboat casino in Indiana.

1937 Flood in Evansville

While doing research in August 2013, I called my long-time friend Janice (Rech) Kroeger who was born and raised in Evansville.   While visiting her one summer she had taken me through the Evansville Museum of Arts, History and Science and shown me some of her father's incredible photography.   His name was Ed Rech (pronounced "wreck"). The original footage he shot of the flood and its aftermath, much of it from a Coast Guard boat, was donated by his family to the museum.   Ed and his wife had two

Evansville Flood, January and February of 1937.

children, Janice and Bill. Both are still living. Janice and her family still live in Evansville.

The Dress Plaza, Evansville Flood, January 28, 1937.

Janice married Ron Kroeger over 60 years ago so she is no longer a "wreck"! Ron and Jan retired to Evansville where they were both born and raised. So all of the "first-hand" information about Evansville came from them.   Jan also put me in touch with Tom Lonnberg who is the Director of the Evansville Museum of Arts, History and Science and he provided me with the two photographs which are included in this chapter. Both are clearly identified as Ed Rech's work.   The one identified as "Dress Plaza" shows the date taken (3:15 P.M. Jan. 28, 1937) and water at 53.13.

EF3 Tornado of November 6, 2005

On November 6, 2005 an EF3 tornado struck Evansville, Indiana, killing 25 people and injuring about 230. It was amazing how people responded to help the victims. The coordinating officer for FEMA noted, " I don't think I've ever seen a community come out so quickly to help each other. All communities come together after a disaster, but this one is exceptional."

Summary

Tom Lonnberg, Director of the Evansville Museum of Arts, History and Science provided me with the two pictures taken by Ed Rech of the 1937 Evansville Flood. Evansville can be very proud of its museum.

In spite of its being Indiana's third largest city, Evansville has retained much if its small-town friendliness and charm.

Deadly Tornado Outbreak of 2012 in Indiana

On March 2-3, 2012 a violent EF4 tornado outbreak occurred. In Indiana its primary targets were the small towns.

In Marysville, population 1,900, it virtually flattened the town. Fortunately, there were no fatalities.

In Henryville, population 1,905, there was extensive damage and three fatalities.

In New Pekin, population 1,401 there were 11 fatalities. A 15-month-old toddler was scooped up by the tornado and swept into a field. She died two days later in Kosair Children's Hospital in Louisville, Kentucky. Her parents and two siblings had been killed instantly. All of the family members were buried in two coffins in a nearby paupers cemetery. What a grim reminder to us all that we should never complain and whine about trivial things.

CHAPTER EIGHT

IOWA

History

The first Europeans to visit the area were the French Explorers Jacques Marquette and Louis Joliet in 1673. The United States obtained control of the area in 1803 as part of the Louisiana Purchase, and during the first half of the 19th Century there was heavy fighting between the settlers and the Indians.

Iowa was organized as a territory in 1838.

When Iowa entered the Union on December 28, 1846, as the 29th state, the Capitol was Iowa City. Des Moines became the Capitol in 1857, and at that time the state's present boundaries were drawn.

Iowa produces a tenth of the nation's food supply. Its farms lead the nation in all corn, soybean and hog marketing. The state comes in third in total livestock sales.

Iowa has experienced nearly every type of natural disaster. The following are some of the worst.

Drought and Heat Wave of 1936

Farms throughout the Midwest were devastated by the deadly drought and heat wave of 1936, and Iowa was no exception. Crops withered and died in the fields. Grasshoppers and chinch bugs devoured anything left. There were no crops to sell. There was no money so people lost their farms and their homes. They went hungry. Neighbors helped each other as best they could. At that point in time there was no crop insurance, etc. When the rains finally came in September and October, it was too late to save the crops.

Floods of 1993

The flood of 1993 covered large areas of the upper Midwest but Iowa was the center of it. Flooding resulted in 17 fatalities and more than $2 billion in damage.

500 Year Flood of June 2008

Nearly one-third of Iowa was under water. A disaster proclamation was issued for 83 counties. In Cedar Rapids alone approximately 4,000 homes had to be evacuated.

A levee on the Des Moines River burst, forcing the evacuation of more than 200 homes in north-side neighborhoods and flooding North High School.

Interstate 80 was closed in both directions. Union Pacific Railroad bridge washed out at Waterloo.

Cedar Rapids, Iowa, during the flood of June 2008.

Parkersburg, Iowa, Tornado, May 25, 2008

The town of Parkersburg, population 1,900, was hit by a deadly EF5 tornado on May 25, 2008. Seven people were killed, 350 homes were destroyed, and another 100 suffered minor damage.

Davenport, Iowa, Fire of January 7, 1950

The deadliest fire in Davenport history occurred on January 7, 1950. Forty-one people died at St. Elizabeth's Hospital, a mental ward operated by Mercy Hospital. Most of the fatalities were female patients trapped behind windows locked shut by rusty iron bars. The cause of the fire was attributed to a patient who set fire to the curtains with a cigarette lighter.

Iowa Snowstorm of March 10-14, 1951

It was a bizarre spring moisture-laden snowstorm that lasted four days with the majority of the snowfall occurring on the first day, March 10th. Over 27 inches fell in Iowa City, setting a record for Iowa. No deaths were attributed to the storm.

Ice Storm of February 23-25, 2007

A crippling ice storm occurred in northeast Iowa in late February 2007. There were some reports of ice two inches thick. Gusting winds over 50 miles per hour made matters worse, bringing down tree branches and power lines along with power poles. At the height of the storm as many as 265,000 people were without power.

Summary

It is hard to find a place more "America Heartland" than Iowa. It is the only state whose east and west borders are formed entirely by rivers – the Mississippi River on the east, the Missouri River and the Big Sioux River on the west.

CHAPTER NINE

KANSAS

History

Meriwether Lewis and William Clark explored the Louisiana Purchase territory along the Missouri River in 1804. When the Kansas-Nebraska Act was passed in 1854, the Kansas Territory was opened up for settlement.

The Homestead Act of 1862 offered citizens federal land for a small fee and their promise to live on and improve the land for five years.

In 1899, in Medicine Lodge, Kansas prohibitionist Carry Nation (having left her first husband, Dr. Gloyd, because of his alcoholism) decided she would become "The John Brown of Prohibition." History doesn't tell us what happened to Dr. Gloyd nor the hatchet Carry Nation used to smash liquor bottles in saloons!

In 1917 the demands of World War I brought an agriculture boom to Kansas. The demand for wheat was astonishing. Farmers were paid record prices. During the war the land produced millions and millions of bushels of wheat and corn which helped to feed America as well as numerous nations oversees.

Then in 1918-1919 the world-wide influenza pandemic killed more people than World War I. Kansas was no exception. A fifth of the world's population was infected.

In the early 1930s Kansas as well as the other Great Plains states was a victim of the "Dust Bowl."

In 1993 floods damaged or destroyed one-fifth of the Kansas farmland.

BAXTER SPRINGS, KANSAS

The city of Baxter Springs, population 4,238, was incorporated in 1868 and is the most populous city of Cherokee County. Its beginnings were as a trading post and it was the first "cow town" in Kansas following the Civil War. Its population grew dramatically in the early 1870s. After railroads were constructed into Texas, cattle drives were no longer made to Baxter Springs, and the town declined.

Then on July 6, 1895, a deadly tornado laid waste to Baxter Springs. Six people were killed instantly, several others were fatally injured, and scores were fatally injured, maimed, and crippled. Historical records show that the Methodist Church was in existence in 1895 since two different storm tracks collided near the church. The resilience of the people was amazing. They rebuilt.

First United Methodist Church, Baxter Springs, Kansas.

The First United Methodist still exists today. A photo I took Saturday, May 25th, 2013, is included herein. The beautiful brick building is large and appears to be quite new. People from this congregation traveled to the First United Methodist Church in Joplin, Missouri, immediately after Joplin's tornado of May 22, 2011, to lend assistance.

In the early twentieth century the discovery of lead in the tri-state area revived the economy of Baxter Springs. Years later with the decline of lead mining, the city took another downturn.

In 1926 the downtown Main Street became a part of historic Route 66 which connected Chicago to Los Angeles. Once again Baxter Springs bounced back.

When I was conducting research for this book, my husband and I stopped for coffee and a pastry at a cute little restaurant downtown where locals encouraged us to go over to the Baxter Heritage Center and Museum. At the museum, we discovered that the extensive collection of material from the defunct Picher, Oklahoma, museum had been relocated and lovingly displayed in Baxter Springs' museum.

Baxter Springs is alive and well. People look out for one another. And they are very welcoming to visitors. Can't beat that Midwest hospitality.

Baxter Springs is located about 13 miles west-southwest of Joplin, Missouri. And the incorporated area of the city extends to the Kansas-Oklahoma state border.

FRONTENAC, KANSAS

Frontenac was established in 1886 as a coal mining town. The population was 3,437 as of the 2010 census. It was a part of Cherokee-Crawford Coal Fields and drew a large part of its workforce from European immigrants.

Mining Disaster

The mining disaster that occurred November 9, 1888, killed 44 men and boys. Two of the boys who died were only 13 years old. The explosion occurred when a miner setting explosives accidentally ignited dry coal dust which exploded a full keg of gunpowder. Additional kegs of gunpowder then exploded. It was the worst mining disaster in Kansas history.

Employees of Mine No. 9 Between Pittsburg & Frontenac, in 1906.

Economic Collapse

The economic collapse following Black Thursday in 1929 began the decline of the coal market. And at the end of World War II, the mines closed.

Survival of Frontenac

Two things contributed to Frontenac's survival: (1) its location where it is a convenient drive to major cities such as Pittsburg, Joplin, Kansas City and

Springfield; and (2) it has preserved its ethnic roots in its local businesses and social activities.

GREENSBURG, KANSAS

History

Greensburg is the county seat of Kiowa County and is located in the south-central part of the state. As of the 2010 census the population was 777. Greensburg was named for D.R. "Cannonball" Green who owned a stagecoach company and who helped form the city.

Greensburg is also home to the world's largest hand-dug well.

EF5 Tornado

At 9:45 p.m. CDT on May 4, 2007, Greensburg was hit by an EF5 tornado which destroyed 95 percent of the town and severely damaged the other 5 percent. Eleven people were killed. Tornado sirens sounded 20 minutes before the tornado struck, which undoubtedly saved many lives.

The S.D. Robinett Building, the only historic building in downtown Greensburg to survive the tornado

UDALL, KANSAS

History

Udall is a small town in Cowley County, Kansas. It was founded in 1881 by J. M. Napier and P. W. Smith, and was named after English author Cornelius Udall. Its population as of the 2010 census was 746.

Udall Tornado

The worst tornado in Kansas history leveled the small sleeping community of Udall on May 25, 1955, at around 10:30 p.m.   The south half of town was completely leveled.   All of the houses except one in the north half of town were damaged.

The only remaining businesses were the bank, the post office, and the Odd Fellows Home.   Gone were 192 buildings and 170 homes.   The remaining homes were found unlivable.

But the real tragedy was the loss of lives.   Buildings could be replaced; lives could not.   Eighty-seven lives were lost.   Nearly half of the families of Udall lost one or more members.   Approximately 200 were injured. Twenty percent of the population of Udall was gone.

The aftermath of the Udall, Kansas, tornado of May 25, 1955.

Summary

Out of the rubble and despair emerged not only a new Udall but improved communication of severe weather.   We cannot change the weather, but we can be better prepared so as to minimize the risk.

WICHITA, KANSAS

History

For many years Wichita served as a meeting place and trading center.   In 1863 the first permanent settlement of Wichita Indians was recorded.

J. R. Mead was the first white settler.   He opened a trading post and established the area as a base for the Chisholm Trail.   The city of Wichita was incorporated in 1870. It became a destination for cattle drives from Texas and was nicknamed "Cowtown."   When new rail lines moved west so did the cattle trade, and Wichita fell on hard times.

Wichita bounced back in the 1890s when grain replaced cattle in the economy of the area.

When a great oil reserve was discovered nearby in 1918, the population of Wichita nearly doubled. Oil money allowed local entrepreneurs Lloyd Stearman, Walter Beech, and Clyde Cessna to further develop Wichita's fledgling airplane industry. Wichita boomed and still today Wichita produces more than 40% of the world's general aviation aircraft.

Wichita's rise from a "cowtown" to the largest city in Kansas required vision, not only by the entrepreneurs named above but by many others as well. McConnell Air Force Base was established in 1941. Its primary mission is to conduct air refueling and airlift globally when and where needed. McConnell is located four miles southeast of the central business district of Wichita. McConnell is still active today.

On April 26, 1991, an EF5 tornado devastated many of the facilities at McConnell but missed a line of B-1B bombers and the maintenance hangers.

And on January 16, 1965, a KC-135 refueler took off from McConnell. It crashed into a Wichita neighborhood a few minutes after take-off, killing 30 people. Among the dead were seven crew members. The cause of the crash was engine failure. It was Wichita's largest aviation disaster.

CHAPTER TEN

KENTUCKY

History

In 1750, Dr. Thomas Walker led the first documented expedition through the Cumberland Gap. In 1769, Daniel Boone ventured through the Gap to begin settlement of the Bluegrass Region. In 1792 the Commonwealth of Kentucky became the 15th state.

In 1809, Abraham Lincoln was born near Hodgenville.

The great majority of early Kentuckians were farmers. They grew most of their own food. They used the corn crop to feed hogs and to distill into whiskey. Their cash came from selling tobacco, hemp, horses and mules.

Tobacco was a labor intensive crop, and plantations in the Bluegrass Region used slave labor.

Kentuckians loved horses. Breeding thoroughbreds for racing is a Bluegrass specialty. Louisville began sponsoring the world-famous Kentucky Derby at the Churchill Downs track in 1875. Actually, it was called the Louisville Jockey Club at that time and was later renamed Churchill Downs. The first derby was run on May 17, 1875.

Mules were cheaper to own than horses. Mule breeding was another specialty of Kentuckians, and many of the mule breeders moved west to Missouri to expand their operations.

Coal Mining

Around 1750, Dr. Thomas Walker was the first recorded person to discover and use coal in Kentucky.

53

In 1820 the first commercial mine, known as the McLean drift bank, opened in Kentucky near the Green River and Paradise in Muhlenberg County. Kentucky has been mining coal ever since. Many Kentuckians made the change from subsistence farming to coal mining, especially in the Appalachian region.

Coal companies built "coal patch" or "coal camp" villages and towns near their coal mines throughout Kentucky and other coal mining states. The coal company generally provided for churches and schools to be built. Company-owned stores for provisions, etc., were also built where employees could buy on credit.

"Sixteen Tons" is a song about the life of a coal miner, first recorded in 1946 by American country singer Merle Travis. According to Travis, the line from the chorus, "another day older and deeper in debt" was a phrase often used by his father, a coal miner himself. This and the line, "I owe my soul to the company store," is a reference to the truck system and to debt bondage. Under this scrip system, workers were not paid in cash; rather they were paid with non-transferable credit vouchers which could only be exchanged for goods sold at the company store.

U. S. Coal and Coke Company coal processing plant, Lynch, Kentucky.

This made it impossible for workers to store up cash savings. Workers also usually lived in company-owned dormitories or houses, the rent for which was automatically deducted from their pay. In the United States the truck system and associated debt bondage persisted until the strikes of the newly formed United Mine Workers and affiliated unions forced an end to such practices.

Feuds and Violence

Kentucky saw it all: violent feuds (especially in the mountains) between clans, political fighting which resulted in the assassination of Governor Goebel, and Ku Klux Klan violence. Prohibition led to widespread bootlegging.

The Great Depression

In the late 1920s the Great Depression led to widespread unemployment and severe hardship. New Deal programs greatly improved the educational system and led to the improvement of infrastructure. The creation of the Kentucky Dam and its hydroelectric power plant greatly improved the lives of Western Kentuckians.

The Ohio River Flood of 1937

Beginning in January 1937 the Ohio River was in various flood stages for three months. One-third of Kenton and Campbell Counties were submerged, and 70% of Louisville was under water for over a week. Paducah, Owensboro and other Purchase area cities were devastated.

LOUISVILLE, KENTUCKY

History

Louisville was named in honor of Louis XVI of France. It is the largest city in Kentucky, with a population of 253,128. The town's charter dates back to May 1, 1780.

Disaster Struck Louisville

The great flood of the Ohio River in 1937 changed Louisville forever. Ninety people lost their lives, and 175,000 were evacuated from their homes. The Ohio River rose to 30 feet above flood stage. In some places in Louisville, the Ohio River was 24 miles wide.

To make matters worse, the Louisville Varnish Company caught fire, killing three people.

After the flood, the Army Corps of Engineers built a 29-mile flood wall around the city. People moved away from the river. The community came together and rebuilt. But Louisville was forever changed. On

A dead horse drowned in the Ohio River Flood of 1937 is found in a tree near Louisville once the water recedes.

a bright note, even though Churchill Downs had been flooded, the Kentucky Derby ran on schedule in May.

WEST LIBERTY, KENTUCKY

In March of 2012, four tornadoes hit Eastern Kentucky, killing 19 people. No building was left untouched, and few were recognizable.

Deadly Ice Storm of 2009

The worst natural disaster in Kentucky's history was a deadly ice storm in late January 2009. The hardest hit areas were in Western Kentucky. At the height of the ice storm 700,000 residences were without power. 100,000 were without power for over a week. Kentucky Governor Steve Beshear called up the entire Kentucky Army National Guard to deal with the after effects of the storm.

Kentucky Ice Storm damage in 2009 resulted in 700,000 residences without power.

Summary

Barbara (Branson) Brooks can tell you what made rural Kentuckians strong: faith in God, strong work ethics, family, and friends. Her parents, grandparents, great-grandparents, three "old maid" aunts, and one uncle are all buried in a church cemetery in Graves County, Kentucky, about half-way between Murray and Mayfield. The old church building is gone; so is the old one-room schoolhouse.

Barbara was an only child and was expected to work alongside the folks. It made her the strong self-reliant person she is today. She is grateful for the "creature comforts" she now enjoys but has not forgotten her humble beginnings. In fact, she journeyed back this year to visit the old cemetery.

CHAPTER ELEVEN

LOUISIANA

History

Louisiana has been governed under ten different flags beginning in 1541 with Hernando de Soto's claim of the region for Spain.

Almost every nationality on earth is a part of Louisiana's culture. As part of their French legacy, counties are called "parishes," and Law in the state of Louisiana, which is unique among the 50 states, is based in French and Spanish civil law with some common law influences. Ironically, it was the Spanish who built many of the colonial structures in the "French Quarter" in New Orleans, which is Louisiana's largest city. But the Capitol of Louisiana is Baton Rouge.

When President Thomas Jefferson negotiated the Louisiana Purchase in 1803 with Napoleon, he nearly doubled the size of the United States (for $15M). Later, 13 states or parts of states were carved out of the Louisiana Purchase territory.

The plantation economy was shattered by the Civil War. The "Magnolia State" underwent a radical change.

Then, with the discovery of sulfur in 1869 and oil in 1901, coupled with the rise in forestry, came a new wave of economic growth. Eventually, Louisiana became a major American producer of oil and natural gas and a center of petroleum refining and petrochemicals manufacturing.

Cajun Country contains twenty-two parishes and its principal city is Lafayette.

Louisiana has been hit by many hurricanes throughout its history. In 2005, TWO hurricanes, Katrina and Rita, devastated the entire Gulf Coast region.

Hurricane Katrina – August 23-30, 2005

This Category 5 hurricane hit numerous states but the worst devastation was in New Orleans. The final death toll was 1,836.

Katrina wasn't the worst hurricane in United States History. The hurricane on September 8, 1900, in Galveston, Texas, took 6,000 lives – more lives than all the other hurricanes in the United States combined.

Katrina captured the media attention of the entire world and help poured in from all parts of the globe, but the immediate problems were almost overwhelming:

- Communication difficulties and language barriers
- Confusion over the chain of command
- Looting and vandalism
- Fraud and scams
- Health risks from unsanitary conditions, e.g. water contamination
- Trauma and health problems

On a positive note, in addition to the various governmental agencies, non-profits and churches responded with much-needed, "roll up your sleeves" help. It would be impossible to list them all. Cultural and sports organizations stepped up to the plate. For example, Canadian singer Celine Dion donated one million dollars to New Orleans recovery.

New Orleans has a long way to go in their recovery. They still have a lot of obstacles to overcome. But many volunteers are still there today, lending them a helping hand.

Flooded I-10/I-610 interchange and surrounding area of northwest New Orleans and Metairie, Louisiana.

Cajun Country, Louisiana – Flood of 2011

For the first time in 37 years, the Morganza Spillway was opened on May 14, 2011, deliberately flooding 4,600 square miles of rural Louisiana to save most of Baton

Rouge and New Orleans. Fortunately, no loss of life was reported but millions of dollars in property damage occurred.

Hurricane Isaac – August 2012

59,000 homes were damaged by Hurricane Isaac. The storm's worst harm was in St. John the Baptist Parish where nearly one in four owner-occupied houses sustained more than $20,000 damage. Hurricane Isaac came ashore near the mouth of the Mississippi River.

Hurricane Isaac may not have had the most powerful winds the Gulf Coast has ever known, but it moved so slowly through communities in many states that its force was perhaps more frightening than Hurricane Katrina.

LaPlace, La., September 13, 2012 – Volunteers from Samaritan's Purse International Relief install tarp to keep rain from a home damaged by Hurricane Isaac.

CHAPTER TWELVE

MICHIGAN

History

Michigan was admitted to the Union on January 26, 1837, as the 26th state. Its Capitol is Lansing, and its largest city is Detroit.

Michigan has the largest fresh-water coastline of any political subdivision in the world. It is bounded by four of the five great lakes.

The birth of the automotive industry began in Michigan. Ransom E. Olds, John and Horace Dodge, Henry Leland, David Dunbar Buick, Henry Joy, Charles King and Henry Ford all had a hand in transforming Michigan's economy.

Henry Ford no doubt had the biggest impact with his use of the moving assembly line. And productivity increased dramatically with his Model T Ford. He was quoted as saying "You can have any color you want as long as it is black!" The horse and buggy days were gone.

Detroit flourished. They couldn't build housing fast enough as people migrated to where jobs were waiting. That was over a century ago and now the city of Detroit is in Federal Bankruptcy Court filing "Chapter 9."

DETROIT, MICHIGAN

People flocked to Michigan, especially Detroit, where jobs were available. Detroit couldn't build housing fast enough to accommodate the influx of people. And Detroit boomed.

In the summer of 1951 between my junior and senior year in high school, I talked my folks into letting me take a Greyhound bus to Detroit where my Aunt Veda and

Uncle Jim Brooks were both employed in the automobile factories. I was only 16 but I was confident I could find work of some kind, and Aunt Veda and Uncle Jim were delighted to have me there for the summer. They had a big wide closet door in the living room which you opened, and a "Murphy bed" pulled down. To me that was quite a novelty.

I quickly found employment doing housecleaning for working folks. And I loved the streetcars. It cost a quarter to ride one, and you could get a piece of paper called a transfer and go all over. Problem was, being a green country kid from Missouri, nobody told me you couldn't go back over that same route with a "transfer."

Damage from the Beecher, Michigan, tornado, June 9, 1953

So when I boarded a homeward bound streetcar the conductor said "That will be 25 cents please." I didn't have a quarter. I was scared to death! An elderly black man waiting to board behind me stepped up and said, "I will pay her fare." What a wonderful, kind man. I thanked him over and over but I didn't even get his name. It was a lesson in human kindness from a total stranger of a different race, a lesson I will never ever forget.

I'm sure the Detroit of today is nothing like the Detroit of that summer of 1951. That Detroit was a vibrant place where work seemed to be plentiful. Today Detroit is bankrupt.

Flint-Beecher Tornado

An EF5 tornado hit Flint, Michigan, on June 8, 1953. The tornado moved east-northeast two miles north of Flushing and devastated the north side of Flint and Beecher. The tornado first descended about 8:30 p.m. on a humid evening near a drive-in movie theater that was flickering to life at twilight time. Motorists in the drive-in began to flee in panic, creating many auto accidents on nearby roads.

The tornado dissipated near Lapeer, Michigan. Nearly every home was destroyed on both sides of Coldwater Road. Multiple deaths were reported in 20 families, and it was reported that papers from Flint were deposited in Sarnia, Ontario, Canada, some sixty miles east of Flint.

Large sections of neighborhoods were completely swept away, with only foundations left. Trees were debarked and vehicles were thrown and mangled. One hundred and sixteen were killed, making it the tenth deadliest tornado in U.S. history. The death toll was surpassed by the tornado of May 22, 2011, in Joplin, Missouri.

The Flint-Beecher tornado is also one of only four EF5 tornadoes ever to hit in Michigan. Another EF5 tornado would hit in Hudsonville, Michigan, on April 3, 1956.

Hudsonville Tornado of April 3, 1956

This EF5 tornado killed at least 17 people and injured 340 in one hour's time, between 6:30 and 7:30 p.m. on April 3, 1956.

CHAPTER THIRTEEN

MINNESOTA

History

In 1819, Fort St. Anthony (later renamed Fort Snelling) was built. Then in 1844 iron ore was discovered in the Mesabi Range.

Then Minnesota became the 32nd state on May 11, 1858.

Deadly Blizzard of November 11, 1940

Minnesota wasn't the only state struck by this deadly blizzard. Nationwide, 150 people died, 49 of them were in Minnesota.

Nobody was prepared. Meteorologists had not anticipated anything like what happened. November 11th began as a beautiful day. Gardens were still producing vegetables. It was a holiday. Duck hunters were elated. Armistice Day held a promise of perfect weather for duck hunting.

By afternoon the "perfect day" took an ominous turn. Winds came up, and the storm grew to hurricane force. At first it was rain, then it turned to sleet, and then snow.

In the blizzard, a freight train and a passenger train carrying duck hunters collided head-on near the Watkins Depot. At the Mobil Station in Watkins a 20-year-old employee, Wendelin Beckers, heard the crash. The train whistle was jammed, and he struggled through the blizzard to the train depot. Residents of Watkins formed a human chain and got the train passengers to safety. Those duck hunters were lucky they were not already out in the wetlands. Many of those perished.

In the midst of the storm a young pianist from Milwaukee began a concert at the College of St. Teresa in Winona, Minnesota. The loud roar of the storm was drowning out his music. But as he started to leave the stage, the audience urged him to keep on playing. He finally concluded his concert by playing "Night Winds." At that time the young pianist was merely known as Walter Liberace of Milwaukee. He is known around the world today by his last name only – Liberace.

Duluth, Minnesota Flood – June 17-20, 2012

Duluth experienced one of its worst floods on record. No lives were lost but 250 residents were forced to evacuate their homes.

Menahga, Minnesota Wildfire – May 2013

A wildfire near Menahga burned 7,100 acres in May 2013. No lives were lost but 12 residences, two commercial properties and 41 other structures were destroyed.

Rochester, Minnesota Tornado – August 21, 1883

This estimated EF5 tornado was one of a series that hit Southeast Minnesota that day. But the Rochester tornado was so devastating that the others were largely overlooked by the press and little is known about them.

Damage from the tornado of August 21, 1883, that struck Rochester, MN.

One unusual occurrence in Rochester during the storm: chickens, absolutely devoid of their feathers but otherwise unharmed, were found wandering around on Broadway! Also, a wooden plank was driven through the trunk of a tree.

The Rochester tornado will be forever remembered: it was the impetus for the creation of the world-famous Mayo Clinic. At least 37 deaths and over 200 injuries were recorded.

Let's back up before we talk about the Mayo Clinic, which wasn't founded until 1889.

Dr. William Worrall Mayo emigrated from England to the United States in 1846, and he became a doctor in 1850. He moved to Rochester in 1864 to examine recruits for the Union Army during the Civil War. He remained in Rochester after the war ended.

Dr. Mayo's two sons, Will and Charlie, got their very early training observing and later assisting their father. Will graduated from the University of Michigan Medical School in 1883. Charlie graduated from Chicago Medical College of Northwestern University in 1888. Both returned to Rochester and joined their father's practice.

When the tornado hit in 1883, temporary hospital quarters had to be set up in offices and hotels. Nuns from Sisters of St. Francis served as nurses

The Rochester tornado resulted in at least 37 deaths and over 200 injuries.

since there was no hospital in Rochester. Mother Alfred Moes requested the Drs. Mayo to join forces with the Sisters to build the first general hospital. St. Mary's 27-bed hospital opened in 1889 as a result of that partnership.

With the exploding growth of medical knowledge it became obvious to the Mayos that "individualism" in medicine could no longer exist. They invited other doctors to join with them, and a whole new innovative concept was born. Specialization came into being.

From its humble frontier beginnings Mayo Clinic is world renowned. Its headquarters is still in Rochester, Minnesota, but it now encompasses three clinics and four hospitals in three states.

CHAPTER FOURTEEN

MISSISSIPPI

History

Mississippi was first explored for Spain by Hernando de Soto, who discovered the Mississippi River in 1540. The region was later claimed by France. In 1699, a French group under Sieur d'Iberville established the first permanent settlement in Biloxi.

Great Britain took over the area in 1763 after the French and Indian Wars, ceding it to the U.S. in 1783 after the Revolutionary War.

The main crop in the 19th century was cotton and the industry boomed, as the Mississippi River was used for transportation.

On December 10, 1817, Mississippi became the 20th state. Slave labor was used by the farmers for the operation of the large cotton plantations that were growing steadily. With the election of Abraham Lincoln slavery became a part of history.

The great depression saw thousands of farmers lose their land between 1929 and 1939. This was a downfall for the state. Cotton prices plummeted, leaving many in poverty. New legislation alleviated some of the taxes farmers had to pay which helped the economy resurface.

World War II saw the development of industry, and many farmers were replaced by machines. Industrial development soared, and the opening of a massive oil refinery in 1963 pushed the economy toward success.

HATTIESBURG, MISSISSIPPI

History

Hattiesburg was founded in 1882 by pioneer lumberman and civil engineer William H. Hardy and was named in honor of his wife *Hattie.* The town was incorporated two years later with a population of 400.

Hattiesburg Tornado

On February 10, 2013, a tornado moved along one of the city's main streets and damaged buildings at the governor's alma mater, the University of Southern Mississippi. There were numerous reports of injuries and property damage but no lives were lost.

Damage to alumni housing on the University of Southern Mississippi campus.

Hurricane Katrina, 2005

Despite being about 75 miles inland, Hattiesburg was hit very hard by Hurricane Katrina. About 10,000 structures received major damage of some type. About 80% of the city's roads were blocked by trees, and power was out in the area for up to 14 days. The storm killed 24 people in Hattiesburg and the surrounding area. The city is strained by a large influx of temporary evacuees and new permanent residents from coastal Louisiana and Mississippi towns to the south where damage from Katrina was catastrophic.

JACKSON, MISSISSIPPI

On Thursday, March 3, 1966, an EF5 tornado (referred to as the Candlestick Park tornado) struck Jacksonville killing 58 people.

SHUQUALAK, MISSISSIPPI

A strong storm packing ice, snow and tornadoes struck Shuqualak, a small town of 500 people on April 11, 2013.   There were numerous reports of injuries but no fatalities.

SMITHVILLE, MISSISSIPPI

EF5 Tornado of April 27, 2011

The monster tornado that hit Smithville at 3:45 p.m. on April 27, 2011, was part of a massive string of tornadoes which carved a path of destruction from the Deep South to the Canadian border, hitting seven states, numerous cities and small communities.

In Mississippi, it was the small town of Smithville that took a direct hit. There's not much left of Main Street. Or Town Hall. Or the K-12 school. Victory Baptist Church was wiped out.

There were 34 deaths reported in Mississippi.   Seventeen of those were in Smithville, a small town whose population was 942 as of the 2010 census. The town of Smithville looked like a landfill piled with garbage.

On April 27, 2011, an EF5 tornado hit Smithville, MS, which resulted in 17 deaths from a population of 942.

Phil's Place, the restaurant where retirees used to gather to "solve the world's problems" is gone. But *Mel's Diner* has been rebuilt. Now they talk more about God, faith and grace. They reach out to one another in little ways. Smithville continues to struggle with financial difficulties associated with rebuilding and has had to depend on the local communities to just survive.

But there is a lot of resilience in the people. The EF5 tornado destroyed the town but it did not destroy the town's spirit.

TUPELO, MISSISSIPPI

History

In the early years of the settlement of the town it was named *Gum Pond* because of the numerous tupelo trees which were locally known as black gum trees.

During the Civil War the Union and Confederate forces fought in the area in 1864 in the battle known as the Battle of Tupelo. The town changed its name to *Tupelo* after the Civil War and was incorporated in 1870. The city is best known as the birthplace of Elvis Presley.

EF5 Tornado of April 5, 1936 (Palm Sunday)

In 1936 there was neither high-tech National Weather Service tracking nor warning systems. So Tupelo had mere minutes or even seconds to brace for the storm. The fourth-deadliest tornado in American history leveled 48 blocks of Tupelo killing more than 230 people.

Boxcars were brought in through the help of the American Legion, led by insurance agency owner and Post Commander J.M. "Ikey" Savery.

One of the families that occupied a boxcar said there was a curtain strung across the middle of the boxcar and another family occupied the other end of it.

Tupelo was a small town in 1936, and people were struggling under a Recession-ravaged economy. Help poured in from outside the town. Rebuilding began immediately, and jobs were created. All the churches, especially the Presbyterian and Baptist, came to the immediate aid of the victims.

Today, Tupelo is the seventh largest city in the state and has a population of 35,490.

CHAPTER FIFTEEN

MISSOURI

History

Missouri has had a rich and colorful history. A French trading post was established at St. Louis in 1764. Forty years later (1804) the Lewis and Clark Expedition departed from St. Charles.

Mark Twain

Samuel L. Clemens was born in Florida, Missouri in 1835. He wrote under the pen name of *Mark Twain*. Nothing says Missouri literature like *Mark Twain*. He wrote several award-winning American classics.

The Pony Express

In 1860 the Pony Express began its famous run from St. Joseph, Missouri, to Sacramento, California, a distance of 1,966 miles. Normal time was 10 days but its quickest run was 7 days and 17 hours when the riders were carrying President Lincoln's Inaugural Address. The Pony Express ended its service when the telegraph was completed in 1861.

Harry S. Truman

Harry S. Truman, 33rd President of the United States, was born in Lamar, Missouri, on May 8, 1884. On April 12, 1945, following President Roosevelt's death and as Roosevelt's vice president, Harry Truman was sworn in as President. After reelection in 1948, he served his full term but decided not to run for a third term in 1952. When President Eisenhower was sworn in, President Truman retired to Independence, Missouri. He died on December 26, 1972.

Birthplace of the Interstate Highway System

The Interstate Highway System has often been called the "Greatest Public Works Project in History."

In 1956, President Dwight D. Eisenhower signed the Federal-Aid Highway Act. On August 2, 1956, Missouri became the first state to award a contract with the new interstate construction funds.

Gateway Arch in St. Louis

The St. Louis riverfront was chosen by the federal Government in 1935 as the location for a national monument in honor of the early pioneers who explored America west.

St. Louis, Missouri: The world famous Gateway Arch, a 630-foot-high monument.

The Gateway Arch was eventually built in 1965 by Finnish-American Eero Saarinen. It is a monument to the territorial expansion westward. It is one of the most-visited tourist attractions in the world. At a height of 630 feet it is the tallest monument in the United States. It soars high above the Mississippi riverfront and is a marvel in engineering.

The dimensions of the two legs of the Gateway Arch have an interesting history. Both legs were simultaneously constructed and when it was time to connect them together at the apex it created a thermal expansion problem during architectural alignment. The St. Louis Fire Department came up with a novel idea and sprayed the south leg with water until it had cooled to the point where it could be aligned with the north leg.

New Madrid, Missouri, Earthquakes of 1811-12

The series of four earthquakes that occurred beginning December 16, 1811 (two on that day, six hours apart), then the subsequent quakes on January 23, 1812, and February 7, 1812, remain the most powerful earthquakes ever to hit the Eastern United States in recorded history.

New Madrid, Missouri, is a small community in the "boot heel" located on a bend in the mighty Mississippi River. According to U. S. Geological Survey, Reelfoot Lake (on the Tennessee side of the river) was formed when the Mississippi River flowed backwards for several hours. Much of Reelfoot Lake is nothing more than a swamp. It is noted for its bald cypress trees and nesting pairs of bald eagles.

In 1811-12 the Richter scale for measuring the strength of earthquakes had not even come into use so historians can only estimate the quakes' strength. But aftershocks were felt as far away as Quebec, Canada. Because the earthquakes hit in a sparsely populated area there were no known fatalities.

Great Flood of 1993

The flooding of the Mississippi and Missouri Rivers and their tributaries in 1993 not only affected Missouri, it affected Illinois, Iowa, Kansas, Minnesota, Nebraska, North Dakota, South Dakota and Wisconsin as well. The flood was among the most costly and devastating to ever occur in the United States, with $15 billion in damages.

Summary

There are so many small communities and towns in Missouri that I couldn't write about them all. But as a native daughter I still think of Missouri as HOME. I am so thankful to God that I had the privilege of growing up in rural Ripley County. Nobody bothered to lock their doors. Neighbors helped each other. Cypress Creek School was a one-room school house where Grades 1-8 were taught and kids walked to school. Discipline was allowed, and I received my fair share of it. Then when I got home I got it again! Not too surprising since I had four older brothers who at one point were attending that school.

A Bookmobile, which was a "library on wheels," came out from Doniphan once a month. Kids were allowed to check out a limited number of books which had to be returned when the Bookmobile next arrived.

Of course the old Cypress Creek School is long gone and now the kids are bussed to a centralized school in town.

When I returned home to attend my 60th high school reunion in Doniphan in 2012, we found our way over to the Center Hill Baptist Church. It is still going strong.

Sunday mornings when we were growing up, the entire family dressed in their "Sunday Best" and attended Center Hill Baptist Church. First one there got to pull the rope to ring the church bell which hung in the belfry and called folks to worship.

The Ten Commandments are still displayed on the wall. Comfortable pews have replaced the old hard wooden benches. A young man with a beautiful voice played a newer piano. But they still have old hymnals with the wonderful songs I grew up with. Church attendance was very good. They have added a wing onto the old structure which they use for Sunday School and other functions.

JOPLIN, MISSOURI

History

If you are a history buff, a visit to the Joplin Museum Complex in Schifferdecker Park is a must. Brad Belk is the Executive Director, and his very knowledgeable assistant, Bonnie, will be happy to help you.

Let's go back to the 1830s. Reverend Harris G. Joplin, a Methodist circuit rider preacher, made his way to southwest Missouri. He planted a Methodist congregation in the new frontier. The town was eventually named after him.

The discovery of lead deposits in Joplin Creek Valley occurred even before the Civil War, and a few mining camps sprung up. It is possible that part of the Battle of Pea Ridge, Arkansas, was to gain access to the lead mines near Joplin. Missouri was a Union state, and the Confederacy needed lead for ammunition. And Joplin isn't all that far from Pea Ridge. The Confederacy lost the Battle of Pea Ridge.

Zinc deposits, which were more valuable than lead, were discovered, and after the Civil War ended numerous mining camps sprung up. Mining became the dominant industry in the Joplin Valley for decades.

While the mining camps brought enormous wealth, they also brought an undesirable element as well. Violence and frontier lawlessness abounded. No history of Joplin would be complete without mentioning the famous three-story *House of Lords.* The saloon and restaurant were on the first floor, gambling was on the second floor, and the brothel was on the third floor. No doubt a LOT of money changed hands on all three floors!

Resident John C. Cox filed a plan for a city on the east side of the valley and named it *Joplin City.* The nearest sheriff was in Carthage across the valley.

Carthage resident Patrick Murphy filed his plan for a city on the other side of the valley and named it *Murphysburg.*

Eventually the two cities merged into *Union City.* But the merger was found to be illegal so the two cities split. Murphy suggested that a combined city be named *Joplin* and that merger was successful. So on March 23, 1873, *Joplin* became a city.

When the price of zinc collapsed after World War II, Joplin was by then diversified enough to weather the downturn in the economy, thanks to its central location. And when the famed Route 66 was built linking Chicago to Los Angeles it went right through Joplin.   Then when the Interstate highway system was built in 1958, Interstate 44 ran just south of Joplin.

Joplin – Civil War Involvement

Need for lead for bullets and shot was vital. The Tri-State Mining District (also called the Joplin Region because financial, manufacturing, and transportation industries that served the district centered in Joplin) was of utmost importance to both Union and Confederate forces.

One of the reasons for the battle in Pea Ridge, Arkansas (just below the MO-ARK state line in northwest Arkansas), was an attempt to take control of the lead mines in Joplin.

The fierce battle was an important victory for the Union but 5,949 lives were lost; 4,600 of those were Confederate soldiers.

The Tornado

Joplin is situated in "Tornado Alley" and had experienced tornados in the past. However, on May 22, 2011, it was hit by the "Granddaddy of them all" – an EF5 tornado which resulted in 164 deaths and more than 900 injuries. Several books have been published about that deadly tornado. The first books cited 161 deaths but according to Bonnie at the Museum three more people died of tornado related injuries.

Recovery

Father Jon-Stephen Hedges of Isla Vista, California, was deployed to Joplin by the Red Cross immediately after the tornado hit. He was no stranger to disaster areas. He was Chaplain to the Santa Barbara Sheriff's Department. He had been deployed by the Red Cross to New Orleans when Katrina hit. In fact, he arrived in New Orleans ahead of the Red Cross so he reported in to the Police Department to lend assistance. He had also served as a first responder during Hurricane Ike in Galveston, Texas (September 2008), so he was a "seasoned veteran" when it came to working in disaster areas.

Father Jon-Stephen Hedges

Father Jon's comments about Joplin, Missouri, were heart-warming: "I came away from Joplin with the conviction in my heart that this was a city that was going to make it. In addition to the people of Joplin and the surrounding area rolling up their sleeves and working side by side, during the two weeks I was there I saw vehicles with license plates from all across the United States there to help. What a blessing!"

After talking with Father Jon I was determined to write about Joplin but I had to finish up with my first book.

On October 19, 2012, we were finally able to travel to Joplin. Father Jon had told us that if we liked Greek food and got to go to Joplin, we should go to *Mythos* restaurant on Rangeline Road. *Mythos* had escaped being hit by the tornado. We went there for dinner, met George Michalopoulos, and enjoyed the best Greek food we had ever tasted. And while there we met Clyde Stout who overheard us telling George that we were from Santa Maria, California.

Clyde had been stationed at what is now Vandenberg Air Force Base (which is only about 19 miles from Santa Maria) in the 1950s. We exchanged phone numbers, mailing addresses, and e-mail addresses. We kept in touch and were able to return to Joplin on May 25, 2013.

The Spirit Tree, Joplin, Missouri

The *Spirit Tree* is a tornado-damaged tree that stands near where Dillon's Grocery store stood prior to the storm. It was painted vivid bright colors by local artists to lift people's spirits and has become another tornado landmark.

Photograph by Clyde Stout

The Spirit Tree, Joplin, Missouri.

Joplin Mural

Residents of Joplin painted a huge mural to tell the story of the Joplin tornado. *Spiva Center for the Arts* mounted an exhibit of works created to help repair the physical and emotional scars left by the storm.

Photograph by Clyde Stout

Joplin Mural, the story of the Joplin tornado.

Joplin Mentor – Clyde Stout And His Wife Donna

God answered a prayer on my first research trip to Joplin in October of 2012. Clyde and Donna were having dinner at Mythos restaurant on Rangeline Road. Father Jon-Stephen Hedges of Isla Vista, California, had told us that if we got to Joplin, since both of us loved Greek food, to go to Mythos and to meet George, the owner.

George came out of the kitchen and we told him we were from Santa Maria, and that Father Jon had sent us. We had quite a conversation before he had to go in the back in the kitchen.

Clyde and Donna were seated at the closest table to ours. Clyde asked, "Did I hear you say you were from Santa Maria?" We found out he had been stationed at Vandenberg AFB which is about 19 miles from Santa Maria.

Clyde and Donna Stout, of Joplin, MO, were our mentors and guides while in Joplin.

The restaurant was getting a bit noisier so we asked Clyde to roll his wheelchair to our table. Donna had said she had some errands to run so she would see Clyde later. I wondered how he was going to get home if she was leaving!

My husband asked Clyde if he had lost his leg in the tornado. He said no, he had lost his leg in 2004. He has lots of big picture windows, and he had seen the tornado from the big window in his kitchen.

People were waiting to be seated so we exchanged phone numbers, e-mail addresses, etc., and promised to keep in touch.

It was seven months before we were able to return to Joplin. In the meantime a strong friendship had developed. On our return trip in May 2013 we had arranged to meet them at their church on Sunday and attend services together.

After church they ""rolled out the red carpet" for us. Since they knew their way around Joplin, Clyde suggested we leave our car in the church parking lot and ride with them in Clyde's extended cab truck.

I was in awe at the way Clyde popped the tonneau cover on the back of his truck, collapsed his wheelchair and hoisted it into the truck in one smooth maneuver. So much for my concern the year before about how he was going to get home!

They took us to their favorite Chinese restaurant for lunch. The food was wonderful and so was the conversation. Then they took us on a tour of the areas where the tornado had struck. I didn't have my notebook with me so I tried to commit everything to memory. Impossible!

Not to worry. Clyde took pictures later of the rebuilding going on and mailed me the memory stick from his camera. Included in this chapter are a few of his photos. I wish I could have displayed them in color but that is cost-prohibitive.

Photograph by Clyde Stout

St. Mary's Cross, Joplin, Missouri, withstood the forces of the tornado.

Clyde had seen the tornado from his large kitchen window. At first it was just this greenish cloud, and there was lots of hail. Afterwards he could see the horror left behind. It looked like a war zone. The pictures you saw on TV didn't do it justice. The people who could do so rolled up their sleeves and began digging in the rubble to find people and help. All Clyde could do was sit in his wheelchair and pray.

Clyde provided me with the cell phone number of Fred Mason. I talked to him on the phone. When he and his family came out of their basement all they had left were the clothes on their back. There is a separate article on the Masons.

Clyde also gave me the name and phone number of his aunt, Betty Snodgrass, in El Reno, Oklahoma. Her story is in the Oklahoma chapter of this book. Clyde was born in El Reno and spent a lot of time at her house when he was a kid.

Clyde is from a small but closely-knit family. He has one sister, Margaret. She and her husband live about 25 miles from Joplin at the head of Beaman Hollow. Their elderly parents (dad is 94, mom is 96) live about a mile from Margaret.

Donna was born and raised in Goodman, Missouri, which is about 25 miles from Joplin. She has four brothers who all still live in the local area.

Clyde and Donna have one son, Todd, his wife Wendy, and two granddaughters: Samantha (16) and Jessica (13). They are very blessed.

Joplin Tornado Survivors - Fred and Kathy Mason

Here is the Masons' story, told in their own wonderful heartwarming words:

> Fred and Kathy Mason and their oldest daughter, Jessica, and five-year-old grandson Jordan (who were visiting) were at Fred and Kathy's tri-level home when the EF5 tornado hit Joplin on May 22, 2011. They raced down to the lower level and put Jessica and Jordan in the closet under the stairway. Fred and Kathy took shelter in the bathroom a few feet from the closet. Lady, their dog, thought Kathy was heading back upstairs so she headed that direction. Kathy screamed for Lady to come and barely pulled her into the bathroom as Fred was trying to close the door. The force was so strong when the window burst that it sent glass and debris flying towards them. With all their strength they managed to shut the door and hold it shut. From inside the bathroom they heard the debris pelting against the door and the house ripping apart. When they all came out of our refuge places, we saw we were all safe but Fred and Kathy had lost everything except the clothes on their backs. Jessica had lost her car which she had just purchased a few weeks before. They praised God that they were still alive and started the process of getting to safety as natural gas was spewing out of the meter.

> Fred and Kathy's second oldest daughter, Erin, lived across town. Erin and Shawn (her fiancé – now her husband) and their daughter Isabella (18 months) along with three other adults had barely gotten into a small bathtub in the center of their home when the house exploded. They felt two tugs on the bathtub and then they were airborne inside the tornado. The bathtub with five adults and one small child flew 300 feet down the road and then dropped to the ground. They had debris piled on top of them so they had to dig their way out. The five adults had cuts and bruises but Isabella did not even have a scratch on her. They had lost everything but praised God that they had made it through. They started looking for a way to get out of the area to safety.

Faith, their third oldest daughter, had been to an outdoor wedding west of town. The wedding ended early due to the weather changing and she was driving home. It was getting darker and darker and hailing hard as she moved forward towards home. Her car stalled at a stoplight, and Faith prayed that God would help her to start it and get her to safety. Her car started, and she turned it around and went up into a subdivision that had already been hit to take shelter in a home where she knew the owner. She stayed there for a while and then started to try to make her way home again, not knowing how far or how much damage had been done to Joplin. She was unable to advance in the direction she wanted to go due to a temporary triage. It was then she learned that the Joplin High School had been destroyed. Knowing that her parents lived a few blocks from there, she was worried that she had lost her parents in the tornado. It took five hours and several phone calls to finally reach a relative (Uncle Rick) in Illinois to find out that Fred and Kathy, as well as her sister and nephew were okay. Faith stayed at a friend's parents' house (Randy) that night which was close to Interstate 44.

Fred and Kathy's youngest child and only son, Michael, lived north of town. He and his wife's home was not in the path of the tornado. They came into the devastation to pick up Fred, Kathy, Jessica and Jordan. They then planned to pick up Erin, Shawn and Isabella. Due to downed power lines, debris in the roads and other destruction, they were unable to get to them. They found out that Erin, Shawn, Isabella and the three other adults had found shelter for the night in in the home of a doctor who took them in, treated their wounds, fed them, and got diapers for Isabella.

Michael and his wife, Alicia, opened their home up to us to stay while we got situated. They also opened up their garage to store donations that people were sending from all over. Most of these items were collected by Joshua Mason, Fred's nephew, who lives near Moore, Oklahoma.

After everyone was accounted for and in a safe place, Michael and Jessica set out looking at every hospital and shelter they were told about, looking for Kathy's sister, Sally Moulton. Sally had been at the Stained Glass Theatre (next to St. John's Hospital) finishing up the final performance of *I Remember Mama* when the tornado sirens went off. At three o'clock in the morning they reported to Fred and Kathy that they had to get a few hours of sleep and would start searching again. The next morning Faith heard from Randy that the Stained Glass Theatre had been destroyed, and there had been two casualties. Randy's daughter broke the news to Faith that her Aunt Sally had been one of the casualties. Faith called her uncle Rick in Illinois and broke the news to him about his sister, Sally.

Joplin is a town full of people that has a human spirit like none other. They care for one another. They help one another. And they bond in strength that comes from God who gives and takes away.

Fred has a nephew, Joshua Mason, who lives in Moore, Oklahoma. Joshua and his family loaded up a bunch of supplies and brought them to Fred after the tornado struck. When Moore got hit with a deadly tornado on May 20, 2013, Fred returned the favor by hauling supplies down to his nephew.

Fred is a board member of the Joplin Tornado Response Board. He says it is so heartwarming the way people have come together to rebuild Joplin. Groups from out of the area continue to come in. The Response Board arranges for housing and meals. In fact, when I spoke with him on the phone on July 27, 2013, he said that a group of 13 people, mostly high school and college students, were arriving the next day to help with building housing.

Branson, Missouri Tornado

A tornado struck Branson on February 29th (Leap Day) of 2012. Branson is a small town (population of around 10,000) tucked away in the Ozarks of southwest Missouri. Packed with a huge number of big show theaters owned by many well-known live entertainers, it is little wonder that it attracts over a million visitors each year.

The Branson tornado did quite a bit of property damage, but no lives were lost and only minor injuries occurred. Fortunately it struck in the off-season time.

In spite of its small size, Branson people immediately came to the aid of Joplin in their time of need when an EF5 tornado struck May 22, 2011. According to Taylor Pruitt, people from Branson made the 110 mile trip up to Joplin with loads of supplies. Another person (I didn't get his name) said he went up and worked with a group who took chainsaws, picks, shovels, etc. to help clear debris.

Kansas City, Missouri Floods

The Great Flood of 1951 on the Missouri River was the most devastating of all Kansas City floods because the levee system was not built to withstand it.

It completely destroyed the Kansas City Stockyards which were second only to Chicago stockyards in size. It also caused the Kansas City International Airport to be built far away from the Missouri River bottoms to replace the heavily damaged Fairfax Airport in Kansas City, Kansas.

The Great Flood of 1993 was not as devastating to Kansas City because of levee improvements after the 1951 flood.

Kansas City is the largest city in Missouri and is located only 157 miles north of Joplin. So when the EF5 tornado hit Joplin on May 22, 2011, it was able to respond quickly and in a big way. Their major sports teams (Kansas City Royals, Kansas City Chiefs) contributed in a big way with money and labor.

Missouri Ice Storm, 2009

Missouri is no stranger to ice storms but the storm of January 2009 was an ugly one for Southeast Missouri. All of the towns and rural areas in the Bootheel were devastated. Around 100,000 people were without power.

More than 2,500 power poles and hundreds of transmission lines were downed, cross-arms were broken and poles snapped. The electric cooperatives throughout the state pitched in but the amount of skilled utility personnel needed was overwhelming. Other states that could do so also helped, but this same storm hit the state of Kentucky even harder.

Also, the need for supplies such as power poles, transmission lines, etc., was staggering, and Missouri had to turn to other states for assistance.

Volunteers were wonderful. They came in with chainsaws and helped to clear debris and to get food and assistance to homes, etc. but the Missouri electric cooperatives had the heaviest burden.

Besides the immediate pain of getting communities and rural areas back on line, utility companies in some of Missouri's poorest counties wonder where they will get the millions of dollars they estimate they will need to virtually rebuild their entire networks.

The wonderful infusion of help from electric cooperatives from Missouri, Iowa, Louisiana and Mississippi did not go unnoticed; a church sign off south I-55 said *God Bless Utility Workers.*

St. Louis Tornado History

The St. Louis metropolitan area has a long history of tornadoes. In fact, more tornado fatalities have occurred in St. Louis than any other city in the United States. Yet in spite of their own tornado woes, St. Louis came to the aid of Joplin "big time" when an EF5 tornado struck on May 22, 2011. Individuals, churches, nonprofits, sports teams (such as the St. Louis Cardinals, St. Louis Rams, St. Louis Blues), and the city itself all pitched in to help Joplin.

The 1896 St. Louis-East St. Louis tornado injured more than 1,000 people and caused at least 255 fatalities.

A deadly tornado struck St. Louis in September 1927. Then in April 2011 an EF4 tornado struck the northern part of the St. Louis metropolitan area causing widespread damage (but no fatalities), including significant damage to Lambert International Airport. It caused a complete shutdown of Lambert for over 24 hours.

CHAPTER SIXTEEN

MONTANA

History

Montana is located in the northwestern United States. It has the distinction of sharing a 545-mile border with three Canadian provinces: British Columbia, Alberta, and Saskatchewan. It is the fourth largest state and is the largest landlocked state.

Montana was admitted to the Union on November 8, 1889, as the 41st state. One of its nicknames is "Big Sky Country."

Montana contains Glacier National Park, "The Crown of the Continent," and portions of Yellowstone National Park, including three of the park's five entrances.

Cattle ranching has been an important part of Montana's history and economy since the 1850s. Wheat farms in eastern Montana are also major producers of high quality wheat.

Climate

Montana has a greatly varied climate. The coldest temperature on record for the state is also the coldest on record for the contiguous 48 states. On January 20, 1954, -70 degrees Fahrenheit was recorded at a gold mining camp near Rogers Pass.

The area west of the Continental Divide has milder winters, cooler summers, less wind, and a longer growing season.

BUTTE, MONTANA

Granite Mountain Copper Mine Disaster – June 8, 1917

The most deadly hard-rock mining disaster in United States history was at the Granite Mountain copper mine near Butte, Montana.   168 miners died in the disaster.

The flame from a foreman's carbide lamp started the fire when he went to inspect an electric power cable that had been damaged when it was being lowered into the mine. The power cable carried electricity to the underground pumps.

The fire quickly traveled up the cable turning the mine shaft into an inferno and trapping the miners below. The mine was at full wartime production. 213 miners escaped through levels connecting to other mines.

Of the miners who died, most died from asphyxia. Some did not die immediately; they wrote notes while waiting to be rescued. A few barricaded themselves within bulkheads and were found about 55 hours later. A strike followed the mine disaster.

In Butte, Montana there is a memorial to the miners who died in the mine.

Violence in Butte

Violence erupted in Butte, Montana, less than two months after the mine disaster. The violence was not just from the disaster but from Anti-WWI vs pro-war advocates; immigrants, many of who were German and anti-WWI; radical unions; disputes with Native Americans; etc., all of which came into play. It was an explosive environment just waiting for something to light the fuse.

Union organizer Frank Little (Industrial Workers of the World) arrived in Butte less than two months after the mine disaster intending to organize the miners. His anti-WWI inflammatory speeches resulted in his being dragged from his boarding house by masked vigilantes on August 1, 1917, and hanged from a railroad trestle. The National Guard was sent to Butte to restore order.

1918 Influenza Epidemic

A year after the mine disaster and the ensuing strikes and violence, an influenza epidemic broke out which claimed the lives of over 5,000 Montanans.

An economic depression began in Montana after World War I and lasted through the Great Depression until the beginning of World War II.

World War II and Montana

The national economy was in bad shape in 1941 and Montana was no exception. Even before the United States entered World War II on December 7, 1941, many Montanans had already enlisted to get away from the poverty. Another 40,000 entered the armed forces the first year of the war and more than 57,000 entered before the war ended.

Native Americans from Montana entered the armed services in large numbers. "Code Talkers" from the Crow Nation were a tremendous asset to the military.

One Code Talker, Barney Old Coyote, joined the Army Air Corps at the same time as his older brother, Henry. Barney was only 17 and was allowed to serve with his older brother. Barney, a tail gunner in a B-17 bomber, was allowed to break radio silence while flying over North Africa and Europe to speak freely with his older brother Henry in his native Crow tongue. He was one of the most decorated World War II Native Americans, earning 17 decorations for his marksmanship and a title of WWII Flying Ace. Both he and his older brother survived WWII.

Barney Old Coyote, a Native American and member of the Crow Nation, earned 17 decorations in WWII as a Code Talker and a gunner in a B-17.

WWII brought jobs to Montana as military installations sprung up. Air bases were built in Great Falls, Lewistown, Cut Bank and Glasgow.

Post-WWII Era

In the post-WWII Cold War era, Montana became host to U.S. Air Force Military Air Transport Service (1947) and, eventually, the Strategic Air Command (1953) based at Malmstrom AFB in Great Falls.

Hebgen Lake Earthquake of 1959

The main residence of Hilgard Lodge is almost wholly submerged in Hebgen Lake after the August 17, 1959, Yellowstone National Park earthquake. A portion of State Highway 287 also was swallowed up by the lake.

The largest earthquake recorded in the Rocky Mountains shook southwest Montana and sent the side of a mountain crashing down over a campground. At least 28 people died and many were injured.

The main residence of Hilgard Lodge is almost completely submerged in the Hebgen Lake following the August 1959 Hebgen Lake (Montana-Yellowstone) earthquake.

CHAPTER SEVENTEEN

OHIO

History

Marietta, Ohio, was the first permanent American settlement in the Northwest Territory. Ohio became a state on March 1, 1803. The Capitol of Ohio is Columbus.

The "Mother of Modern Presidents," Ohio, was the birthplace of seven U.S. presidents: Ulysses S. Grant; Rutherford B Hayes.; James Garfield; Benjamin Harrison; William McKinley; William H. Taft; and Warren G. Harding.

Ohio's state motto is WITH GOD ALL THINGS ARE POSSIBLE. In 1997 the American Civil Liberties Union (ACLU) filed a lawsuit against Ohio, claiming that the motto violated the First Amendment to the U. S. Constitution which ensures freedom of religion. A Federal ruling determined that since the motto did not endorse a specific God, it was not a violation of the First Amendment. Ohio retained its motto.

Ohio is known as the "Birthplace of Aviation" because the Wright Brothers, John Glenn, and Neil Armstrong were all born in Ohio. The first airplane (which Wilbur and Orville Wright flew) was constructed in Ohio.

CLEVELAND, OHIO

Tornado – June 8, 1953

The population of Cleveland was just over one million in 1953. Tornadoes were reported by visual sightings since Doppler radar was not yet in use. Because the tornado occurred in the early evening, it was upon the city rather quickly.

This was an EF4 tornado so it packed a lot of destructive power. The property damage was in the millions of dollars. Incredibly, only nine people were killed but many were injured.

National Guard patrols were brought in to protect property. Doctors and nurses at local hospitals had to work by flashlight to treat the injured because of power outages.

MOSCOW, OHIO

Tornado of March 4, 2012

This EF3 tornado which struck Moscow, a small village of 185 people, leveled the village. One person, Councilwoman Carol Forsee, was killed when her house was flattened.

Residents and volunteers immediately pitched in. Pastor Ralph Ollendick of the River of Life Church brought 100 people from his congregation on Sunday. Instead of holding a church service, they brought chainsaws, rakes, shovels or whatever they could to help clean up the devastation. This was a shining example of "people helping people."

XENIA, OHIO

History

Xenia (pronounced ZEEN-ya) is a city in Green County in southwestern Ohio about 21 miles from Dayton. The population as of the 2010 census was 25,719. The name comes from the Greek word "xenia" which means hospitality.

Moscow, Ohio, tornado damage in 2012.

Dr. Michael J. Young, my optometrist in Santa Maria, California, was born and raised in the north-central part of the United States. He told me about Xenia, Ohio's terrible tornado so I pursued its history.

Xenia was founded in 1803, the year Ohio was admitted to the Union. The friendly, growing young town soon attracted many pioneer industries – flour mills, sawmills, woolen mills, pork packing plants, oil mills, and tow mills. The town grew rapidly during the mid-19th century.

Tornadoes

Xenia has a long history of severe storm activity. In fact, the Shawnee Indians referred to it as "the place of the devil wind" or "the land of the crazy winds." On April 3, 1974, an EF5 tornado cut a deadly path directly through the middle of Xenia, killing 34 people (including two Ohio National Guardsmen), injuring an additional 1,150 people, destroying almost half of the city's buildings, and leaving 10,000 people homeless. Five schools, nine churches, and 180 businesses were also destroyed. People poured in from other communities to lend assistance, and the city's plight was featured in the national news. Comedian Bob Hope (who had grown up in Cleveland, Ohio) organized a benefit for Xenia. In appreciation, the new Xenia High School Auditorium was named "Bob Hope Auditorium."

Courtesy of National Oceanic & Atmospheric Administration
The Xenia Tornado of April 3, 1974,
as it comes through the town.

CHAPTER TWENTY

OKLAHOMA

History

The Indian Appropriations Act of 1889 opened the door for white settlement in America's Indian Territory. On November 16, 1907, Oklahoma became the 46th state to enter the Union. The name *Oklahoma* is derived from the Choctaw phrase *okla humma* literally meaning "red people."

Often people tend to think of Oklahoma as flat and barren. But it has four primary mountain ranges: the Ouchita Mountains, the Arbuckle Mountains, the Wichita Mountains, and the Ozark Mountains.

The United States acquired the land which is now Oklahoma as a part of the Louisiana Purchase in 1803 from France. Oklahoma's capitol and largest city is Oklahoma City.

"During the 19th century thousands of Native Americans were expelled from their ancestral homelands from across North America and transported to the area including and surrounding present-day Oklahoma. The phrase 'Trail of Tears' originated from a description of the removal of the Choctaw Nation in 1831 from the southeastern United States. But the term is usually used for the Cherokee removal." (Len Green. "Choctaw Removal was really a 'Trail of Tears'." Bishinik, mboucher, University of Minnesota.)

Discovery of oil in the 20th century led to rapid growth in population and wealth. Tulsa, especially, benefitted from this infusion of wealth.

In 1927 an Oklahoma businessman, Cyrus Avery, known as the "Father of Route 66," began the campaign to create U. S. Highway 66. It all began in his hometown of Tulsa, and, eventually, the famous *Route 66* ran all the way from Chicago to Los Angeles.

A farmer and his two sons during a dust storm in Cimarron County, Oklahoma, 1936, Photo: Arthur Rothstein.

During the 1930s parts of Oklahoma, especially the Panhandle, began suffering the consequences of extended drought, poor farming practices, and high winds. The term "Dust Bowl" not only applied to Oklahoma but extended to the areas of Kansas, Texas, Colorado and New Mexico as well as other states. The Dust Bowl Days forced thousands of farmers into poverty and caused Oklahoma's greatest migration, many to farming communities in the Central Valley of California.

Tri-State Lead and Zinc Mining District

We had gone through the huge Mining and Mineral Museum in Joplin in the autumn of 2012 so on Saturday, May 25, 2013, we decided to venture out from Joplin and explore the old mining towns that were within easy driving distance.

Our first stop was Galena, Kansas, which advertises itself as "the oldest mining town in southeast Kansas." Galena's Main Street was part of the historic Route 66, and in its heyday Galena had a population of 30,000. It is now around 3,000. The most interesting site near Galena was the old Eagle-Picher Plant. This smelter processed locally-mined galena ore and produced lead, zinc and silver from around 1912 until the late 1970s. This area was once dubbed "Hell's Half Acre" by the locals. At some point Galena had been nearly flattened by a tornado. Many old buildings appeared abandoned.

Our next stop was Baxter Springs, Kansas. This old mining town is still very much a "going concern." We stopped at the local café for a coffee break. The locals were very friendly – interested and interesting people. They directed us over to their Museum which was terrific. And the material from the abandoned Picher, Oklahoma, Mining Museum is now housed in the Baxter Springs Museum. What a labor of love!

Just a few miles down Route 66 and we were in Oklahoma. Our first stop was the old "ghost town" of Picher. It is a long and sad story about Picher. It is a part of the Tar Creek Superfund Site. There are still a few high chat (tailings) piles that have not been removed. The Government condemned the area and offered buyouts to the residents. The town ceased to officially operate in 2009. The old water tower is still there, and the building that once housed the Picher Mining Museum is fenced and grown up in weeds.

Next we were in Commerce, Oklahoma. There was a care facility of some sort by the highway. The Commerce High School has a large statue of Mickey Mantle out front.

Picher Mining Museum is now abandoned.

Then we arrived at the terminus of our tour – Miami (pronounced *ma-AM-ah)*, population 13,737 (Est. 2012). It was 1:30 p.m. and we were HUNGRY. Went to Montana Mike's Steak House and the parking lot was packed with cars and pickups. Got seated in a booth in the bar and ordered. Soon found out why the parking lot was full – Miami High School was having its 55th Class Reunion in the big banquet room, and they were having fun!

Next time I go to Miami, Oklahoma, I want to the take a tour of the historic old Coleman Theatre, which opened April 18, 1929. It is on the National Register of Historic Places and seats 1,600 people!

Tornadoes in Oklahoma

Oklahoma ranks number one in tornado disasters according to Federal Emergency Management Agency (FEMA). Oklahoma really is the bull's-eye state for awful tornadoes.

Oklahoma is the leading state when it comes to safe rooms which probably saved lives in Moore, according to FEMA.

Moore, Oklahoma Tornado on May 20, 2013

Moore, Oklahoma, population 55,081, which is a part of the Oklahoma City metropolitan area, was struck by an EF5 tornado on May 20, 2013. Neighboring Newcastle and South Oklahoma City were also struck. Damage was extensive, with the destruction of entire subdivisions, along with both Briarwood and Plaza Towers elementary schools while school was in session. The Oklahoma Department of

2013 Moore EF5 tornado damage at Briarwood Elementary School.

Emergency Management reported that 24 people, including 10 children, were killed, 377 were injured, approximately 1,150 homes were destroyed, and there was an estimated $2 billion in damages.

Hours after the tornado the American Legion committed up to $1 million through the Temporary Financial Assistance (TFA) program and National Emergency Fund to assist veterans and their families affected by the storm. As dawn broke the day after the storms, the Legion joined Soldier's Wish on the ground in Moore to provide hot meals for storm victims and relief workers and to help with cleanup and recovery.

El Reno, Oklahoma Tornado on May 31, 2013

El Reno, a city of 16,749, is located about 25 miles west of downtown Oklahoma City. It is located at the interchange of I-40 and U.S. Route 81. The EF3 tornado that struck El Reno was the widest tornado ever documented with an estimated width of 2.6 miles. It killed eight people, including three storm chasers (Tim Samaras, his 24-year-old son Paul, and Tim's colleague, Carl Young), and one amateur storm chaser.

World War II POW Jay Jeffrey from Oklahoma

Jay Jeffrey was born September 13, 1924, in Canadian, Oklahoma, which is a small community about 20 miles north of McAlister. His father was a Cherokee Indian and his mother was Irish.

There were nine siblings: three girls, then five boys, then one more girl. Jay was the oldest of the five boys.

His father worked in the oil fields and shortly before Jay started school the family moved to Oklahoma City. The first day of school he cried and wanted to go HOME.

His early life was a hard-scrabble existence. Picking cotton was one of the worst stoop-labor jobs. His mother was pregnant most of the time. In fact, she gave birth to one of his siblings in the cotton field. The pay was one penny per pound of cotton picked.

Just keeping food on the table was a struggle. Jay doesn't remember having any NEW clothes. He went barefoot most of the year. Both of his parents worked hard and did the best they could for their family.

The Great Depression left the entire nation struggling but Oklahoma was hit especially hard. And the Dust Bowl days really took its toll, especially in western Oklahoma. Steinberg wasn't far off the mark in his book *Grapes of Wrath.*

Jay's father got a job as a meat inspector in Oklahoma City. Times were a little better. Then he developed a hernia and medical care was not very good. Gangrene set in and he died. He was only 63 years old.

Oklahoma City employees had a $1,000 life insurance policy. His mother took the $1,000, packed up the kids and their meager belongings and headed for Yucaipa, California, where she had relatives -- six brothers, four sisters and her mother.

In April 1943 Jay was drafted into the U.S. Army. He was sent to Camp Robertson in Little Rock, Arkansas, for basic training. World War II was in full bloom, and he was shipped overseas to France via Glasgow, Scotland, then England. The trip over was

Jay Jeffrey, originally from Cherokee Nation, Oklahoma, was a WWII prisoner of war in German Prison Camp Stalag C-3.

not bad-- he was aboard the *Queen Mary.* Then his good luck ran out. He was captured in 1943 and spent the next 11 months and 20 days in a German prison camp -- Stalag C-3.

How did he escape? He and four other GIs were sent out with two German guards on a work detail to repair bombed-out roads, which required being gone from the prison overnight. All four of the other GIs were in the Air Force. Their plane had been shot down, and they were captured. One of them was a big Blackfoot Indian about six foot five inches tall named Russell.

They had to sleep in a barn, and the two German guards went to sleep. The Indian rummaged around the barn and found a knife. They devised a scheme where two of the GIs would jump on each of the sleeping guards and pin them down. Then Russell slit their throats. They had to travel by night and hide during the day but they were finally able to reunite with American troops. Even that wasn't easy. The American troops were suspicious and questioned them one at a time until they were sure they were American GIs.

American camps for returning GIs were named after cigarettes. Jay and his other POW buddies were in Camp Lucky Strike. Before returning to the United States Jay and one of his buddies were given a two week R&R in Paris. Jay ended up getting inebriated and came back to the base sporting a tattoo with a girl's nickname on it – *Torch!*

The war was over. Jay came home a decorated hero with no marketable employment skills. After being unemployed for a while, Jay and one of his buddies decided they would join the Air Force. They went to the Recruiting Office in Oklahoma City. They wanted to enlist but they told the recruiting officer they wanted to go to France. He said "Sure, we can do that."

Off they went to Lackland AFB in San Antonio, Texas. At that time 18-month sign-ups were o.k. Needless to say, they did NOT get to go to France, but they did learn some marketable employment skills. And they learned not to believe recruiters.

CHAPTER NINETEEN

TEXAS

History

The Spaniards were the first Europeans to reach Texan shores in 1519. In 1685 the French founded a French colony at Matagorda Bay. In 1716 Spaniards established Catholic missions. And in 1823 Stephen F. Austin built an American colony on the Brazos River.

Texas won its independence from Mexico at the Battle of San Jacinto in 1836. Statehood was granted in 1845.

Texas occupies the south-central segment of the United States. It is the second largest state, only exceeded by Alaska in area.

Six flags have flown over Texas: Spain, France, Mexico, the Republic of Texas, the United States, and the Confederacy – which inspired the name of the amusement park chain, which originated in Texas in 1961.

The first suspension bridge in the United States was the Waco Bridge across the Brazos River built in 1870. It is still in use today as a pedestrian crossing.

In 1900 the deadliest hurricane in U.S. history struck Galveston, killing about 6,000 people. More people died in the Galveston Hurricane of 1900 than the combined death toll of all the hurricanes that have since struck the United States.

Near Beaumont on January 10, 1901, oil was discovered in the Spindletop field. From that point on the oil industry would never be the same again for that "gusher" ushered in the modern age of petroleum.

According to NOAA, the deadliest Texas tornado occurred in Waco, Texas, on May 11, 1953, killing 114 persons.

In 1962, NASA's Johnson Space Center opened in Houston.

In 1963, President Kennedy was assassinated in Dallas.

In 2001, the collapse of Houston-based Enron was the largest bankruptcy in U.S. history.

GALVESTON, TEXAS

History

Jean Lafitte and his pirates established a settlement in 1817, and the town was abandoned and burned when the United States forced Lafitte to leave a couple of years later.

During the Texas Revolution the harbor served as the port for the Texas Navy. By the Civil War, Galveston was Texas' principal seaport and leading commercial center. And by 1890, Galveston was Texas' largest and wealthiest city.

On September 8, 1900, the 38,000 residents of Galveston experienced the worst natural disaster in U.S. history – a hurricane that took more than 6,000 lives and left the city in ruins. Galveston Island was only 8.7 feet above sea level. The 150 mile per hour winds and the 15-foot surge of water easily swamped the island. The wind and water destroyed everything in its path. More people died in the Galveston hurricane of 1900 than the combined death toll of all the hurricanes that have since struck the United States.

The carnage was beyond belief. The bodies of the storm's victims littered a landscape strewn with debris in which few buildings remained standing. Corpses were brought in by wagon loads. They were badly decomposed so the workers took them out to sea in boats but they

Galveston Hurricane, 1900. Workers removing the dead from destroyed buildings.

were washed back to shore. The workers finally had to just burn them on the piles of debris.

Galveston immediately began the task of clean-up and rebuilding. The city raised its buildings by as much as 17 feet by pumping sand beneath their foundations. A thick sturdy seawall was then built along the island's ocean front. But Galveston was never the same. The shippers moved north to Houston's safer harbor.

ST. MARY'S ORPHANAGE

Galveston Hurricane of 1900

On September 8, 1900, the most deadly hurricane to ever hit the United States struck Galveston, Texas. The death toll exceeded the total of all other hurricanes combined.

The most tragic loss of life at any one location was at an orphanage. The following information regarding the orphanage appears on the website of the Congregation of the Sisters of Charity of the Incarnate Word, Houston, Texas, http://www.sisters ofcharity.org. Linda Macdonald, Director of Communications for the Congregation, is responsible for the website. Her grandfather, Clarence LaCoume, was a survivor of the hurricane.

St. Mary's Orphanage before the hurricane of 1900.

Permission to reproduce this story is courtesy of the Congregation of the Sisters of Charity of The Incarnate Word, Houston, Texas.

Legacy: 1900 Galveston Storm

More than 6,000 men, women and children were killed. Among the dead were 90 children and 10 Catholic Sisters at the St. Mary's Orphanage. Only three boys and a hymn called "Queen of the Waves" survived from the orphan's home.

Prior to the Great Storm, St. Mary's Orphan Asylum stood on a beautiful beach just three miles west of the city of Galveston. Established by the Congregation of the Sisters of Charity of The Incarnate Word, the orphanage was home for 93 children and the 10 Sisters who cared for them. The orphanage itself consisted of two large two-story dormitories with balconies facing the gulf. Between the dormitories and the gulf were large sand dunes supported by salt cedar trees.

On the morning of September 8, 1900, rain was falling and the winds were increasing in strength. The island community had experienced many gulf storms before but this one was to change Galveston forever. Around noon Sister Elizabeth Ryan, who had gone into the city to collect provisions, returned to the orphanage. She had declined pleas from the Sisters at St. Mary's Infirmary, a hospital also founded by her Congregation, to stay there until the storm passed.

By mid-afternoon, the waters of the gulf had eroded the sand dunes and approached the front steps of the dormitories. The Sisters brought all the children into the girls' dormitory because it was the newer and stronger of the two. To calm the children, the Sisters had them sing "Queen of the Waves," an old French hymn. The water continued to rise, eventually entering the dormitories. The Sisters took the children to the second floor and again had them sing "Queen of the Waves."

By late that afternoon, the waters of the gulf filled the first floor of the dormitory. In an effort to protect the children, the Sisters tied the orphans to themselves with clothesline. Each Sister tied to herself from six to eight children. It was a valiant, yet sacrificial effort. With winds around 150 miles an hour and a 20 foot storm surge, the sisters and children heard the crash of the boys' dormitory as it gave way to the waters. Again they sang the hymn. Eventually, the girls' dormitory collapsed.

Only three boys were able to escape: Albert Campbell, Frank Bulanek Madera and William B. Murney. The 10 Sisters and 90 children who died in the storm were buried wherever they were found, still tied together.

Despite this great loss, the Sisters of Charity of The Incarnate Word continued their mission and one year later opened a new St. Mary's Orphanage within the city limits. It continued until 1965 when orphanages were giving way to foster homes.

Today our Congregation has spread the ministry of Jesus Christ to communities throughout Texas as well as to Louisiana, Utah and California. In addition, the Congregation has overseas ministries in Ireland, El Salvador, Guatemala and Kenya. Wherever we are in the world, on September 8th we sing "Queen of the Waves." We sing and remember the Sisters, children and all those who faced the incredible tragedy known as the Great 1900 Storm."

NAMES AND NATIONALITIES OF THE 10 SISTERS WHO GAVE THEIR LIVES AT ST. MARY'S ORPHANAGE

Sister M. Camillus Tracy, Superior (31), Irish
Sister M. Evangelist O'Sullivan (33), Irish
Sister M. Elizabeth Ryan (36), Irish
Sister M. Vincent Cottier (45), French
Sister M. Genevieve Davalos (29), Mexican
Sister M. Catherine Hebert (43), Canadian
Sister M. Raphael Elliot (27), Irish
Sister M. Felicitas Rosner (34), German (Alsace)
Sister M. Benignus Doran (23), Irish
Sister M. Finbar Creadon (21), Irish

Galveston Recovery

Long before Hurricane Ike struck Galveston on September 13, 2008, the city had done much to bolster its defenses. Galveston had actually raised its buildings by as much as 17 feet by pumping sand beneath their foundations. A thick, sturdy seawall had been built along the island's ocean front.

Restoration of Victorian neighborhoods has done much to restore the city's beauty. The 32 miles of beautiful sandy beaches and the warm waters of Galveston Bay have always made Galveston a major tourist destination.

Galveston has rebounded from hurricane Ike and sports lots of attractions. Its current population of over 47,000 makes for less congestion and a more relaxed atmosphere, making it a great family place.

GRANBURY, TEXAS

Granbury was founded in the 1860s. It has a population of 7,978 and is located about 37 miles south of Ft. Worth.

On May 15, 2013, an EF4 tornado hit Granbury. In Rancho Brazos Estates, a small subdivision of manufactured homes southeast of Granbury, six people were killed.
Dozens of people were injured. Many were transported to hospitals in the Dallas-Ft. Worth area.

Emergency personnel were quick to respond; 18 bulldozers went into the area "to get people in and to get people out."

Granbury, Texas. Emergency personnel look through debris following an EF4 Tornado that hit on May 15, 2013. *The Associated Press*

This tornado was one of at least 10 confirmed across North Texas that Wednesday night.

GROOM, TEXAS

Cross of Our Lord Jesus Christ

This cross is located 42 miles east of Amarillo on Interstate 40. The cross was built by Steve Thomas of Pampa, Texas in 1995. Mr. Thomas, disgusted with the huge billboards advertising XXX pornography locations on I-40, wanted to make a profession of faith along the Interstate.

Cross of Our Lord Jesus Christ,
Groom, Texas.

Built on private property donated by Chris Britton to avoid legal issues with the ACLU, at a height of 190 feet and weighing 2.5 million pounds, the Groom Cross is reputed to be the second largest cross in the Western Hemisphere. There is a cross in Spain which is taller.

The Groom Cross is visible for about 20 miles. My husband and I had driven by it on I-40 while traveling across the country a couple of times. On October 11, 2012, we stopped so I could tour it.

There are 14 life-size bronze stations of the cross which encircle the base of the cross. There is also a large monument displaying the Ten Commandments.

On a hill west of the cross are three smaller crosses with Christ on the center cross and the two thieves being crucified on either side of him.

There is a building on the east side which houses religious literature and gifts. Free-will donations are gratefully accepted.

The Groom Texas Cross stands as a monument to the fact that God is indeed alive in Texas.

JARRELL, TEXAS

It was by mere coincidence that I heard about the terrible EF5 tornado that struck Jarrell, Texas on May 27, 1997.

On December 26, 2012, I was writing while I was having lunch at *Pepper Garcia's* in the Santa Maria Airport. A tall man in jeans with a piece of carry-on luggage walked in and sat down in the adjoining booth. We struck up a conversation when he asked me where I was traveling to, and I replied that I lived in Santa Maria.

Jarrell, Texas. House foundation swept clean by the tornado at the Double Creek Estates, May 27, 1997.

Since I am inquisitive (that's a polite word for "nosey") I asked where he was traveling to and what brought him to Santa Maria. He was flying back to Austin, Texas. His name was John Groom. He was born and raised in Santa Maria, and he had flown to Santa Maria to spend Christmas with his 91-year-old mother.

He asked me what I was writing, and I told him about my book. He said "You should write about Jarrell, Texas."

He had been with the Sheriff's Department in Jarrell and was on duty when the tornado struck. He took refuge in a culvert which saved his life. The devastation was beyond description. People who were able were digging with their bare hands in the rubble to try to save those trapped.

But the truly amazing part of John Groom's story was that even before the Red Cross got there, in rolled a huge Walmart truck loaded to the brim with all kinds of much-needed supplies. They didn't even bother to inventory the stuff – just got people busy off-loading! How Walmart cut through all the "red tape" to be a "first responder" we will probably never know.

Twenty-seven people perished on that awful day and many more were injured. The scars remain but Jarrell has rebuilt and is still healing.

PORT ARTHUR TODAY

History

The town of "Aurora" at the location of present-day Port Arthur was conceived as early as 1837. The Civil War and the destructive hurricane in 1886 wiped out the town; by 1895 Aurora had become a ghost town. The abandoned community soon became the site of Arthur E. Stillwell's new city, Port Arthur, and was once the center of the largest oil refinery network in the world. And Port Arthur has had a significant air pollution problem.

Port Arthur, Texas. Damage at the docks following Hurricane Ike, September 2008.

In recent history Port Arthur has had to endure Hurricane Rita (2005), Hurricane Humberto (2007), Tropical Storm Edouard (2008), and Hurricane Ike (2008). Hurricane Rita in 2005 struck a direct hit on the Proctor Street Seawall and damaged many downtown businesses and homes.

In addition to the Hurricanes which have ravaged the city for decades, in 2010 the city was the site of an oil spill when an oil tanker and a barge collided causing 450,000 gallons of oil to spill into the Sabine/Neches waterway alongside the city.

People Helping People

You won't find her name in the listing of "Notable residents, past or present" of Port Arthur. She is neither rich nor famous.

Charletha Anderson was born June 8, 1944, in Port Arthur, Texas, to Letha and Charles Henderson. Her given name is a combination of her parents' names.

She was an excellent student at Lincoln High School Port Arthur, graduating in 1962 with a 4.0 GPA. Her goal was to become a registered nurse. She did not have the required prerequisites to enter directly into the 4-year nursing program at Lamar University in Port Arthur, so she worked first as a nurses' aide, then as an LPN, and finally obtained her degree as a registered nurse.

Charletha Anderson, a Registered Nurse and a volunteer,
has spent her life helping others.

Charletha saw history unfold in Port Arthur for the first 58 years of her life. Throughout her childhood she observed first-hand how the people dealt with adversity and reached out to one another. And as a registered nurse she saw unspeakable pain and suffering.

In 2002, Charletha wound up in the very hospital where she worked; she had to have heart bypass surgery. After recovery her doctor refused to release her to go back to her nursing career which she dearly loved.

Undaunted, she called her son in Santa Maria, California, and he encouraged her to move to Santa Maria. She felt well, so she went through numerous tests and passed them all. First she got a nursing job at Cottage Hospital in Santa Barbara. After about a year she was hired by Marian Medical Center in Santa Maria where she worked until she retired in 2010.

Charletha now does volunteer work with cancer patients. The need is great and there aren't enough hours in the day. She is also actively involved with her church. She occasionally fills in as leader of a noon-time Bible study group which reaches out to "working folks" – both "churched" and "ünchurched". Charletha's message is unpretentious and direct: Just believe; Have faith in God; Whatever circumstances you find yourself in, know that God will take care of you; Jesus' love is unconditional; Learn to love each other.

Charletha did take a couple of weeks' vacation in 2012. She flew back to Port Arthur to attend her 50th high school reunion. It was a wonderful, relaxing time. She said a number of the old boarded up buildings downtown had been torn down. New homes were springing up everywhere. Economic recovery seems to be underway for Port Arthur. Finally!

WACO, TEXAS

History

Waco probably derives its name from the Huaco (WAY-co) Indians. Waco was settled in 1849.

Modern Waco is the largest marketing center between Dallas and Austin. The population is 124,805.

Hueco Indian folklore was that Waco would never be struck by a tornado. That proved to be false on May 11, 1953, at 4:36 p.m. when the "grand-daddy of all Texas tornadoes" struck downtown Waco. The tornado was over two city blocks wide. With employees preparing to leave work for the day, they now found themselves crowding into the inner offices of downtown businesses for shelter. Unfortunately, most of the structures in downtown Waco weren't sturdy enough for the impact of the tornado. The 22-story Amicable Life building (now called the Alico building) was newer and made with steel reinforcements and survived intact.

Tom Padgitt building, right, and R. T. Dennis building directly beyond. Here the loss of life was heavy indeed.

There were 114 people who died in the Waco area that day and almost 600 were injured. Twelve of the dead were killed in two cars that were crushed in the street. One of the cars was crushed to only 18 inches tall. Sixty-one of the dead were within one city block between 4th and 5th Streets and Franklin and Austin Avenues.

Bricks and debris from the collapsed structures were piled in the street up to five feet deep. There were survivors who were buried under the rubble for 14 hours, and it took several days to uncover some of the dead from the debris.

Further statistics on the damage:

- $410.2 million in property damage

- 196 businesses and factories were destroyed

- 217 businesses sustained major damage

- 179 businesses sustained minor damage

- 150 homes were destroyed

- 250 homes sustained major damage

- 450 homes sustained lesser damage

- Over 2000 cars were damaged or destroyed

The 1953 Waco Tornado was one of the deadliest in Texas history and was one of the primary factors in the development of a nationwide severe weather warning system.

Waco is the home of Baylor University which was established in 1845 and is the oldest university in Texas; it is also the largest Baptist university in the world.

Otha Jones was born in Gatesville, Texas. His family moved to Waco when he was about four years old. Jo Ann Furneaux was born in Cameron, Texas. Her family moved to Waco when she was 18 months old.

Otha was a junior at Texas A&M, College Station, Texas, at the time of the tornado. He had received his AA in civil engineering at Arlington State

Otha and Blair Jones, formerly of Waco, Texas.

College in Waco and transferred his credits to Texas A&M. He was attending under the Reserve Officer Training Corps (ROTC) program.

At the time of the tornado, Jo Ann Furneaux was a senior at Waco High School. Her father had given her a 1937 Plymouth Sedan when she had gotten her driver's license. She had promptly gone out and wrecked the car. Her father got the body work repaired but he refused to replace the windows which were broken out; the windshield was intact so it was legally drivable.

The day of the tornado it was pouring rain. Several of her friends were going downtown but Jo Ann did not want to get soaking wet by driving downtown with no windows in her car. That decision undoubtedly saved her life.

Gloria Dobrovolny, Jo Ann's classmate, was waiting in the car on the passenger side while her father and another classmate, Barbara Johnson, were in the Pet Store which was next to Rabbit's Pool Hall. Both Barbara and Gloria's father were killed. Gloria survived. The driver's side of the car was demolished.

Otha and Jo Ann were married on December 4, 1954 in her parents' home in Waco. Jo Ann later changed her given name to "Blair." They are now retired and live in Santa Maria, California, where there are no tornadoes!

Waco is still actively reaching out to help those in need. When an explosion occurred at the nearby West Texas Fertilizer Plant killing 14 people including 10 firefighters and paramedics, Waco people were among those first responders who lost their lives. That horrific explosion occurred on April 17, 2013. At this writing the cause of the explosion is still unknown.

CHAPTER TWENTY

WEST VIRGINIA

History

The area which is now West Virginia had a turbulent past. It was a favorite hunting ground for many Native American tribes before the arrival of European settlers. The Appalachian mountains and the beautiful rivers were ideal for their way of life. The Adena tribe had the greatest cultural influence and made many exceptional works of art.

West Virginia was originally part of the state of Virginia but it was never an easy alliance. The western part of the state had very different economic interests. The eastern portion of the state had large plantations, and tobacco was an important crop. They were very pro-slaves, and the western part was mountainous and had little need for slaves. Eventually they split and finally on June 20, 1863, West Virginia became the 35th state.

Harpers Ferry (A Federal Arsenal)

On October 16-17, 1959, John Brown, an abolitionist from Kansas along with 18 armed men, took hostages and freed slaves at Harpers Ferry. None of the slaves would join his campaign and the President sent a unit of U.S. Marines led by

Harpers Ferry

Robert E. Lee to Harpers Ferry. They stormed the firehouse and took Brown prisoner. He was convicted and hanged for treason.

Salt Mining

Even before the Civil War era, West Virginia was a valuable source of salt from its salt mines. But as the salt that could be easily extracted played out, those mines diminished. Newer technology has since proven that West Virginia has enough salt resources to supply the nation's salt needs for about 2,000 years.

Coal Mining

As early as the 1850s, coal was discovered in West Virginia. But there was no feasible way to transport it out at that time. After railroads were built, all that changed.

Monongah Mine Disaster – December 6, 1907

The worst catastrophe in the history of coal mining occurred at Monongah mine six miles from Fairmont, West Virginia. Almost 400 men died.

Monongah, West Virginia, explosion at Fairmont Mining Co. Mine No. 6, December 6, 1907.

At 10:20 a.m. a violent explosion in Mines #6 and #8 completely wrecked both mines and death came instantly to the victims from the spread of deadly gases. The explosion in Mine #8 was so violent that the concrete roof of the engine house was torn in fragments. One piece weighing over 100 pounds was blown more than 500 yards.

The scenes at the mine entrances were pitiful. For several days distraught women gathered near the openings of the mines. They waited and watched and wept. Some prayed. Some shrieked in agony.

Relief work was quick and effective. Additional help was hurriedly brought in from near and far. The mine officials as well as Baltimore & Ohio Railroad company officials took an active part in the relief work. Many acts of bravery were performed by volunteers. With few exceptions there was no need for the physician or rescuer as many of the dead were found sitting upright in the positions they were in when the explosion occurred.

Appeal for funds met with immediate response.   Mass meetings were held throughout the state and beyond. Mr. Andrew Carnegie made a generous donation. The care of the survivors was greatly improved because of this massive effort.

The cause of the explosion will probably never be known.   So complete was the destruction of both mines that there were no surviving miners.

The mines were considered to be the best equipped in the state. The fans at both mines had excellent capacity to force air into the mines. State mine inspector Mr. Larue had inspected them shortly before the disaster and was well pleased with their condition.

Sago Coal Mine Explosion – January 2, 2006

On January 2, 2006, an explosion and collapse of the Sago mine near Buckhannon, West Virginia, trapped 13 miners. Only one of the miners survived. The cause of the explosion remains unknown.

Upper Big Branch Coal Mine Explosion – April 5, 2010

Twenty-nine miners were killed at the Upper Big Branch mine in the Appalachian coal fields. An independent team of investigators from the State of West Virginia wrote a scathing indictment of Massey Energy, owner of the mine. The report said the blast could have been prevented if Massey Energy had observed minimal safety standards.

Summary Regarding Coal Mining

The pages of history are rife with coal mining disasters. And ALL disasters are major to the loved ones left behind. Mining that "old black gold" has put food on family tables for decades.

Mining safety and oversight measures have helped tremendously but mining is still inherently dangerous work. As recently as April 5, 2010, at the Upper Big Branch Coal Mine near Whitesville, West Virginia, twenty-nine coal miners died after a huge explosion occurred.

OTHER WEST VIRGINIA DISASTERS

Buffalo Creek Flood

On February 26, 1972, a mining dam collapsed in Buffalo Creek Hollow leaving 125 dead, around 1,100 injured, seven missing (six of which were infants or toddlers) and over 4,000 homeless. It was one of the deadliest floods in United States history. An earthen dam which gave way after a long period of heavy rainfall was the cause of the flood. Forty of the dead were children.

The Battle of Matewan

The deadliest gunfight in American history occurred on May 19, 1920, in the coal mining town of Matewan, West Virginia. It is often referred to as the "Matewan Massacre." Stone Mountain Coal Corporation owned the mine at Matewan.

John L. Lewis had just been elected President of the United Mine Workers of America. The union was on a roll.

There was no union in the coal fields of southern Appalachia. Miners and their families lived in company-owned houses and required them to buy at the company store.

John L. Lewis was determined to organize the coal fields of southern Appalachia and the union sent in its top organizers. About 3,000 miners signed with the union in the spring of 1920. The coal field operators retaliated with massive firings, harassment and evictions. The independent town of Matewan refused to go along with the coal companies' retaliation against the miners so the coal companies hired their own enforcers – the notorious Baldwin-Felts Detective Agency.

When a contingent of the "Baldwin Thugs" arrived in Matewan, "all hell broke loose." The people of Matewan still argue about who fired the first shot, but when the shooting stopped, the street was littered with bodies from both sides of the battle.

The battle was an integral part of the fight for worker's rights.

CHAPTER TWENTY-ONE

WISCONSIN

History

In 1634, French explorer Jean Nicolet led an expedition ashore near Green Bay. Then in 1673 Jacques Marquette and Louis Joliet traveled through Wisconsin on their journey to the Mississippi River.

In 1783 following the Treaty of Paris, the United States took possession of the Wisconsin Territory.

Wisconsin became the nation's 30th state in 1848.

Peshtigo Fire

On October 8, 1871, a forest fire in and around Peshtigo, Wisconsin, occurred, which, ultimately, became the worst recorded forest fire in North America. The fire spread through Northeastern Wisconsin and Upper Michigan and eventually destroyed property and timberland worth millions of dollars.

The estimated number of lives lost was between 1,200 and 2400. It is referred to as the great Peshtigo fire. The town of Peshtigo, Wisconsin, was completely burned, and 800 lives were lost. Cattle ran into the river to escape the fire. One young girl survived by jumping into the river and holding onto the horn of one of the cattle. People dragged tarps through the water to get them wet, and then took refuge under the tarps. When the tarps were pulled back, the people underneath them had perished, not from the fire but from asphyxiation. The raging fire had consumed the oxygen from the air.

Peshtigo has rebuilt and now has a population of about 3,500. The town is located north of Green Bay.

On that same night, October 8, 1871, the great Midwestern city of Chicago endured their horrific fire.

Tornado Outbreak of Sunday, April 10, 2011

Sunday's outbreak of 10 tornadoes tied Wisconsin's previous record for largest outbreak in the month of April. Total damage and cleanup cost was estimated at more than $20 million. Wisconsin's Emergency Management Team/NOAA/-Wisconsin's Public Services/State Patrol/Red Cross/Salvation Army all worked together in this disaster which covered a widespread area.

Ice Storms

Ice storms are not something people think of when you mention natural disaster. They should.

In March 1976 an ice storm was one of the worst natural disasters to ever hit Wisconsin. Ice accumulations of up to five inches were reported. Power outages were severe. Up to 100,000 people were without power at the height of this storm. The attached photo will give you a sense of its severity.

Ice Storm in Wisconsin, 1974.

Today's Wisconsin

The state has a very diversified economy. Its dairies and cheese are world famous. The beauties of its lakes are awe-inspiring. Its breweries and beer have been around forever. And everyone is aware of its famous football team, *The Green Bay Packers.*

A big note of thanks is owed to three people, without whose help this chapter on Wisconsin could not have been written:

1. **Rusty Kapela** at NOAA in Sullivan, Wisconsin. He not only provided me with information on the tornadoes, he sent me first-hand pictures which he took at the Merrill tornado site.
2. **Joe S. Cordova** of Albuquerque, New Mexico, who was responsible for connecting me with Rusty Kapela. Joe was also the person who brought the

Greensburg, Kansas, tornado to my attention. He and Elaine had driven by that area shortly after it happened.

3. **Elaine Ruth (Hautzinger) Cordova** who was born and raised in Kenosha, Wisconsin. She married Joe Cordova in Denver, Colorado on May 3, 1957, and they raised four wonderful children: John Cordova (wife Diane); Barbara (Cordova) Hurley (husband Lonny); Doug Cordova (wife Amy); and Mary (Cordova) Sullivan (husband Patrick).

BARNEVELD, WISCONSIN

History

Barneveld is a small village in Iowa County, (the southwestern part of the state). The population was 1,231 at the 2010 census.

1984 Barneveld, Wisconsin tornado outbreak

On June 8, 1984, at 12:50 a.m. a powerful EF5 tornado ripped through Barneveld. It was part of a large outbreak of storms which started in the evening of June 7 and touched down in Kansas, Missouri, Iowa and Minnesota.

At the time of the tornado the population of Barneveld was 584. Two hundred residents were injured and nine were killed.

F5 tornado damage in Barneveld, Wisconsin
(Courtesy of NWS Milwaukee)

The town's three churches were flattened. The only remaining and largely undamaged structure was the water tower which had to be repaired and repainted.

Seventeen of the eighteen businesses were destroyed, including all of the government offices, the fire station, library and the post office.

Barneveld Today

Rebuilding began immediately and today the population has more than doubled. Much of that growth may be attributed to its proximity to Madison.

CHETEK, WISCONSIN

History

Chetek is a small town of about 2,221 population in Barron County (northwestern Wisconsin). It was incorporated in 1871. It is on a chain of lakes.

Ice Storms

Since ice storms in the history records seemed to be of counties, not small towns, no detailed information was available on Chetek. There was a one-line entry which indicated that there were eight ice storms recorded between 1950 and 2010.

Tornadoes

I did not find a record of any direct hit on Chetek itself. A tornado hit an area 1.9 miles away from the town. No fatalities or injuries were reported.

The Relaxed Atmosphere of Small Town Life

I first became introduced to the State of Wisconsin in February in the early 1960s. BRR!! I had to drive up from Denver to Chetek to meet with a cousin who owed me money for a car she and her husband had taken to Chetek and smashed into a snow bank.

In spite of the circumstances and the frigid temperature I found myself enjoying the experience. I was able to collect the money from the insurance company down in Eau Claire, sign the "pink slip" over to the cousin on the damaged car and never have to deal with her again.

Then I was able to relax and enjoy the scenery and the people. I was in awe of the people who drove their vehicles out onto the frozen lakes. They didn't just drive them out there, they also had races there! And they built little huts out of blocks of ice and fished on the lake.

The pub by the motel was a fun place to eat in the evening. Entire families came -- all ages. And they all seemed to know each other. It was obvious I was a stranger, but not for long. Everyone was friendly and welcoming. The "blue plate special" was brats and sauerkraut, and I am hooked on those for life.

Then the polka music began. All ages including the kids were out on the dance floor. Before long I found myself drawn out to join in the fun. Some brave soul tried to teach me more intricate polka steps (unsuccessfully, I might add). I headed the car for home the next day with good memories of the people of Wisconsin.

I would enjoy seeing Chetek again – BUT IN THE SUMMERTIME!

MERRILL, WISCONSIN

History

Merrill is in Lincoln County (north central part of Wisconsin). The population as of the 2010 census was 9,661.

Tornado of April 10, 2911

On April 10, 2011, an EF3 tornado struck Merrill. This was part of a powerful outbreak of 15 tornadoes which hit much of the state. The Merrill tornado was the most powerful of the group. The damage was widespread.

Damage from the EF3 tornado that struck Merrill, Wisconsin, in 2011. *(Photo Courtesy of Rusty Kapela.)*

Lutheran Church Charities staff members Pete Imlah and Tim Kurth, along with a volunteer, David Vogeler, drove to Merrill to drop off a Disaster Relief trailer loaded with disaster relief equipment to aid in the clean-up efforts after the tornado that damaged 67 homes in this small town. Before leaving, all three put on their work gloves and began helping clean up debris.

OAKFIELD, WISCONSIN

History

Not much is known about the history of Oakfield. It is a small town with a population of 1012 in Fond du Lac County in southeast Wisconsin.

EF5 Tornado

What is known about Oakfield is that on July 18, 1996, it experienced a massive EF5 tornado that destroyed about half of the community and left hundreds of its residents homeless.

National Guard soldiers were called in to aid victims and clear debris. There was no record of loss of life, but there were numerous injuries and extensive property damage.

There is a one-line reference to destruction of a church and parsonage but I was unable to find out what church it was.

INDEX

Anderson, Charletha 108-109
Ashcraft, Andrew 17
Austin, Stephen F. 101
Avery, Cyrus 95

Bates, Katherine Lee 27
Beasley, Elizabeth 23
Beasley, Evan 23
Beck, Kathi 31
Becker, Bob 16
Becker, Madelaine 16
Beckers, Wendelin 65
Beech, Walter 52
Blecha, Scott 31
Belk, Brad 76
Beshear, Steve 56
Bickett, Tamera 31
Boone, Daniel 53
Brinkley, Levi 31
Britton, Chris 106
Brooks, Barbara Branson 56
Brooks, Jim 62
Brooks, Veda 61-62
Brown, John 113
Browning, Robert 31
Buick, David Dunbar 61

Caldwell, Robert 17
Cameron, Ron 10
Campbell, Albert 104
Carnahan, Mr. 24
Carnegie, Andrew 115
Carter, Travis 17
Cavalier, Robert 39
Cessna, Clyde 52
Clark, William 47
Clemens, Samuel L. 73
Confer, Jan 32
Confer, Larry 32
Cordova, Amy 119
Cordova, Diane 119
Cordova, Doug 119
Cordova, Elaine Ruth Hautzinger 119
Cordova, John 119
Cordova, Joe S. 118-119
Cottier, Sister M. Vincent 104
Cox, John C. 77

Creadon, Sister M. Finbar 104

d'Iberville, Sieur 69
Davalos, Sister M. Genevieve 104
de Coronado, Francisco 27
de la Salle, Sieur 39
de Pineda, Alonso Alvarez 1
de Soto, Hernando 19, 33, 69
de Tonti, Henri 19
Deasy, Father 11
Deford, Dustin 17
Dion, Celine 58
Dobrovolny, Gloria 112
Dodge, Horace 61
Dodge, John 61
Doran, Sister M. Benignus 104
Dunbar, Doug 31
Durand, Asher B. 19

Eisenhower, President Dwight D. 73-74
Elliot, Sister M. Raphael 104

Fleming, Pat 4
Fleming, Philip 4
Flory, Ron 38
Ford, Henry 61
Forsee, Carol 92
Fraijo, Dan 18
Furlough, Thomas 12
Furneaux, Jo Ann 111

Gloyd, Dr. 47
Goebel, Governor 54
Granville, Barbara Beasley 23
Green, D.R. "Cannonball" 50
Green, Emma Edwards 38
Groom, John 107

Hagen, Terri 31
Hampton, David 3-4, 9, 11, 13
Hampton, Heather 9, 13
Hampton, Toni 9, 13
Hampton, Tristan 9, 12-13
Hardy, Hattie 70
Hardy, William H. 70
Hebert, Sister M. Catherine 104
Hedges, Father Jon-Stephen 78

Henderson, Charles	108		Mason, Jordan	82-83
Henderson, Letha	108		Mason, Joshua	83
Holledger, P.C.	22		Mason, Kathy	82
Holtby, Bonnie	31		Mason, Michael	83
Hope, Bob	93		Mayo, Charlie	67
Howard, Eric	31		Mayo, Dr. William Worrall	67
Hurley, Barbara Cordova	119		Mayo, Will	67
Hurley, Lonny	119		McAnulty, Illah Parrish	23
			McDonough, Brendan	17
Imlah, Pete	121		McGary, Hugh	40
			McKee, Grant	17
Jackson, Jason	10		Mead, J.R.	51
Jefferson, Thomas	57		Michalopoulos, George	78
Jeffrey, Jay	98-100		Misner, Sean	17
Johnson, Barbara	112		Moes, Mother Alfred	67
Johnson, Barbara Mills	22		Moulton, Sally	83
Johnson, Marvin	22		Murney, William B.	104
Johnson, Rob	31		Murphy, Patrick	77
Joliet, Louis	43, 117		Napoleon	57
Jones, Blair	111		Nation, Carry	47
Jones, Otha	111		Nicolet, Jean	117
Jones, Ruth Lee	8		Norris, Scott	17
Joplin, Reverend Harris G.	76			
Joy, Henry	61		O'Sullivan, Sister M. Evangelist	104
			Old Coyote, Barney	89
Kapela, Rusty	118		Old Coyote, Henry	89
Kelso, John	31		Olds, Ransom E.	61
King, Charles	61		Ollendick, Pastor Ralph	92
Kroeger, Janice Rech	41			
Kroeger, Ron	41		Parker, Wade	17
Kurth, Tim	121		Parrish, James	23
			Parrish, Katherine Moore	23
LaCoume, Clarence	103		Parrish, Maxine	19
Lafitte, Jean	102		Parton, Dolly	34
Larue, Mr.	115		Percin, John	17
le Moyne, Jean Beinville	7		Pike, John T.	2-3
Lee, Robert E.	113		Pike, Zebulon	28
Leland, Henry	61		Presley, Elvis	72
Lewis, John L.	116		Pruitt, Taylor	84
Lewis, Meriwether	47			
Liberace, Walter	66		Ransick, Lucinda Johnson	21-22
Lincoln, Abraham	53, 69		Rech, Bill	41
Little, Frank	88		Rech, Ed	41-42
Lonnberg, Tom	41-42		Richardson, Helen H.	29
			Rockwell, Norman	19
Macdonald, Linda	103		Roosevelt, President	73
MacKenzie, Christopher	7		Rosner, Sister M. Felicitas	104
Mackey, Don	31		Roth, Roger	31
Maddox, Mayor Walt	10		Russell, Thomas	22
Madera, Frank Bulanek	104		Ryan, Sister Elizabeth	104
Mantle, Mickey	97			
Marquette, Jacques	43, 117		Saarinen, Eero	74
Marsh, Eric	17		Samaras, Paul	98
Mason, Faith	83		Samaras, Tim	98
Mason, Fred	82		Savery, J.M. "Ikey"	72
Mason, Jessica	82-83		Sherman, General	33

Shinn, Mr.   22
Snodgrass, Betty   82
Stearman, Lloyd   52
Steed, Jesse   17
Stephens, Erin Mason   82-83
Stephens, Isabella   82-83
Stephens, Shawn   82-83
Stillwell, Arthur E.   108
Stout, Clyde   78, 80-82
Stout, Donna   80
Stout, Jessica   82
Stout, Samantha   82
Stout, Todd   82
Stout, Wendy   82
Sullivan, Mary Cordova   119
Sullivan, Patrick   119

Thomas, Steve   106
Thrash, James   31
Thurston, Joe   17
Tracy, Sister M. Camillus   104
Travis, Merle   54
Truman, Harry S.   73
Turbyfill, Travis   17
Twain, Mark   73
Tyler, Richard   31

Udall, Cornelius   50

Vogeler, David   121

Walker, Dr. Thomas   53
Walton, Alice   20
Walton, Sam   19
Warhol, Andy   19
Warneke, William   17
Washington, Dinah   8
Wilkinson, Tom   38
Willis, Darrell   17
Woyjeck, Kevin   17

Young, Carl   98
Young, Dr. Michael J.   92

Zuppiger, Garret   17

www.ingramcontent.com/pod-product-compliance
Lightning Source LLC
Chambersburg PA
CBHW050642150426

42813CB00054B/1160

Holiday Wreaths

Christmas Ornament Wreath

Items you will need on hand:

1. Glue gun
2. Glue sticks for glue gun
3. Wire hanger
4. Small Christmas Ornaments (any color)
5. Christmas Ribbon or Bow
6. Pliers
7. Greenery pieces with a stem (2 or 3 pieces)

Directions:

Turn on your hot glue gun.
With the pliers, twist the top part of the hanger until it opens. Bend the wire into the shape of a circle. Add the Christmas ornaments to the wire hanger, until you fill the circle shaped part of the hanger. When you are finished with this part, twist the top part of the hanger back together.

Add some hot glue to the top part of each side of the hanger. Then, add a little to the bottom of the hanger, too! Using the pliers, twist the wire hanger back together. Bend the stems of the greenery, and add them to the top of the wreath. Add a little bit of glue for this step, in case the greenery doesn't stay on the top of the hanger. Add some more hot glue and add the Christmas bow/ Ribbon to the front of the greenery, allowing it to hang down over the greenery. And there you have it!

****Turn off your hot glue gun****

Hanukkah Wreath

Items you will need:

1. Styrofoam Wreath
2. Rolls of blue and silver ribbon
3. 4 inch (thickness) mesh blue and silver
4. Glue gun
5. Glue Stick
6. Silver or blue spray paint
7. Wooden Hanukkah pieces (If you can find them)
8. Floral Pins

Only use the spray paint in a well ventilated room or outside.

Heat the hot glue gun.

1. Spray paint the wooden Hanukkah pieces and let dry
2. Wrap your styrofoam wreath in the ribbon. When you are finished wrapping the styrofoam in the ribbon, add

a little bit of hot glue to the ribbon, just to make sure it will hold tight.

3. Begin using your floral pins and add the mesh (gathering in together) to the styrofoam wreath. Begin on the outer edge. Do that technique around the front, side and back of the wreath.

4. Add mesh to the inside as well.

5. Cut the blue and silver ribbon into 4 inch pieces, and using the floral pins, add them to the mesh. (Add as many pieces as you'd like!)

6. At this point, the wooden pieces should be dry. Use the glue gun to add the wooden pieces to the wreath.

7. Add to your door!

8. ****(Please unplug your hot glue gun.)****

9. Enjoy!

Kwanzaa Wreath

Items you will need for the project:

1. Wreath form
2. Red, black and green ribbon (make sure some have wire in it.) You will need about 10 or 15 rolls of ribbon.
3. Scissors
4. A red, black or green bow

Cut the ribbon into 4 or 5 inch length pieces and put them into piles. Once all of your ribbon is cut, choose which colors that you want, and twist each ribbon piece onto the wreath form. Make sure that they are laying flat, as you add the pieces. Then, you can begin to fluff up the ribbon as the wreath form gets full.
Trim if necessary. And you are finished!

Holiday Ornaments

Glitter, Glass Ornaments

Things you will need for this project:

1. Glass ornaments from the craft show
2. Elmer's glue-- Clear or white will be fine
3. Any color of glitter.
4. Funnel
5. Plastic cup to anchor the ornament when pouring the glue or glitter.

Gently remove the top of the ornament from the ornament, and set it aside.

Lightly squeeze the Elmer's glue into the ornament. Slowly tilt the ornament to make sure that the whole inside of the ornament is covered with the glue. When the glue has covered the inside of the ornament, set your ornament in the plastic cup with the top of the ornament facing up. Get your funnel and insert the funnel into the top of the ornament. Add the glitter to the funnel. Allow enough of the glitter to cover the bottom of the ornament. Then, put a napkin on the top of the open part of the ornament, and gently shake the ornament, so that all of the glitter will cover the glue. When it looks to be fully covered, you can tap the excess glitter, back into the original bottle. Then, you can add the top of the ornament back to the top. And you are done!

Flower Paper Ornaments

Items you will need:
1. Scissors
2. Christmas paper, recycled paper, any type of paper you'd like to make into an ornament
3. Stapler
4. Double-sided,clear tape
5. Colorful thread

1. Cut one piece of 8 1/2" x 11" paper into ½ " strips

2. Make two separate stacks of the strips and staple them; one time in the middle. Fold each stack in half to form two small books.

3. Put a little piece of tape at the tip of the first "page." Then bend it inward toward the center and stick it down. Repeat for every "page" until you have a circular flower shape.

4. Hang with colorful thread.

This is a SUPER easy craft! You can decorate your tree and your whole house with this one!

Pinecone Ornaments

What you will need for this project:

1. Pinecones (any size)
2. Thread
3. Colorful pom poms
4. Hot glue gun with extra glue

Heat up your hot glue gun. Cut an 8 inch piece of thread to the top of the pinecone. Add a tiny bit of hot glue to hold the thread to the pinecone. Decorate the pinecone with the pom poms by adding each pom pom to a dot of the hot glue. (Be very careful doing this. You do not want to get any of the glue on your fingers.) Allow the hot glue to dry, when you are finished adorning each pinecone with pom poms. When the pinecones are dry, you may hang the pinecones around the house.

****(Please unplug your hot glue gun.)****

Table Decor

Snowy Mason Jars

What you will need for this project:

1. Glass Mason Jars (If you want to use plastic jars, do NOT use the glue gun).
2. A can of artificial snow
3. Modge podge
4. Pinecones
5. Craft 'berries'
6. Craft pine (Or natural pine)
7. Hot glue gun with extra hot glue sticks

Heat up your hot glue gun.
Remove the lid of the mason jar, and set it aside.
Open the can of artificial snow. Open the can of modge podge. In the bottom of the jar, add a thin layer of modge podge. Lightly dust the artificial snow into the mason jar. On the side of the jar, add a little bit of hot glue and add the craft pine, craft berries and pinecones. Spray the artificial snow on top of the craft pine, berries and pinecones. Spray a little bit of the artificial snow on top of the mason jar top, and place it back on the top.
All done! You have a beautiful piece of table decor!

****Please turn off your glue gun****

Holiday Cards

Fingerprint Holiday Cards

These are the things you will need for this project:

1. 8x11.5 card stock (Any color you like- However, white or ivory will allow you to use more colors of the paint).
2. Primary colors of liquid tempera paint.
3. A palate for the paint.
4. Your fingers!

This is a fun and easy craft; and depending on how, "perfect" you'd like the cards to be, ask your children to help!

Fold the card stock in half (not long ways). On a palate, add the paint colors that you would like to use. With one finger, dab your finger into the paint, and apply it to the card stock. Make a picture of a tree, or a wreath, whatever you'd like to see! When you are finished, set the card aside to dry. Once your card is dry, you may add a lovely, holiday message for that special someone.

Holiday Appetizers

'Porcupine' Meatballs

Ingredients:

½ cup uncooked long grain rice

½ cup water

⅓ cup chopped onion

½ teaspoon garlic salt

⅛ chopped garlic

1 egg

1 pound ground turkey or chicken (or ground beef)

2 tablespoons canola oil

1 can (15 ounces) tomato sauce

Directions:

In a bowl, combine the first seven ingredients. Mix well. Shape into 1-1/2-in. balls. In a large skillet, add canola oil. Brown meatballs;

about 5-10 minutes on each side. Turn off the stovetop. Drain oil out of the skillet; and set meatballs aside. Add tomato sauce to the skillet. Set the stovetop to your lowest setting. Add meatballs to the sauce. Cover skillet and simmer for 45 minutes. Serve warm. Enjoy!

Turkey Cheeseburger Egg Rolls

Ingredients:

1 Chopped Onion
1 Chopped Garlic
1 pound of Ground Turkey
1 pound of Shredded Cheddar Cheese
4 tablespoons of Sweet Relish
½ cup of Cold Water
Egg Roll Wrappers
4 tablespoons of Canola Oil

Directions:

In a large pan, cook the diced onion, and garlic. Cook for about two minutes. Add the ground turkey to the pan with onions and garlic. Cook meat thoroughly. When the meat is finished, remove meat mixture from the heat, turn off the stove top and set aside. Drain off any excess liquid, and place back into the pan. Sprinkle the cheese and relish into the ground turkey mixture. Stir until the cheese is slightly melted. Remove each egg roll wrapper from the package carefully. Using one wrapper at a time, add about 3 tablespoons of the meat mix to the bottom corner of the wrapper. Tightly roll the wrapper around the filling one time. Fold in the outer corners and continue to roll. To secure the wrapper closed, lightly rub water in each corner, and roll. Repeat this process with the rest of the wrappers until the filling is gone.

Heat another skillet over medium heat. Fill with the canola oil (until about ¼ full.)

Heat the oil to about 350F degrees. Once heated, carefully drop in about 4 egg rolls at a time and fry on both sides for about two minutes or until the outer layer turns a light golden brown on each side. Drain the egg rolls from the oil and place them on a plate with a paper towel or over a cooling rack with a pan underneath. Continue the process until all of the egg rolls have been cooked. Let cool for six minutes before serving.

If you would like a dipping sauce, I would like to suggest a nice ranch dressing!

Garlic Shrimp

INGREDIENTS:

8 tablespoons (1 stick) unsalted butter, cubed
2 pounds extra large shrimp, peeled and deveined
4 cloves garlic, minced
1/4 cup chicken broth
Juice of 1 lemon, to taste
2 tablespoons chopped, fresh basil

DIRECTIONS:

1. Melt 2 tablespoons of butter in a large skillet over medium high heat. Add shrimp. Cook, stirring occasionally, until pink, about 2-3 minutes; set aside.
2. Add garlic to the skillet, and saute, stirring frequently, about 2 minutes. Stir in chicken broth. Bring to a boil; reduce heat and simmer for about 2 minutes. Stir in remaining tablespoons of butter, until melted and smooth.
3. Stir in shrimp and gently toss to combine.

4. Serve immediately, garnished with fresh basil.

HOLIDAY SOUPS

French Onion

- 4 large yellow onions (about 2 pounds), peeled and thinly sliced 4 tablespoons
- 2 tablespoons of canola oil
- 2 tablespoons butter
- 1 teaspoon of sugar
- 2 cloves garlic, minced
- 6 cups of chicken broth
- 1/2 cup of dry white wine
- 2 bay leaves
- 1 tablespoon of fresh thyme (can also use a few sprigs of fresh thyme)
- 8 slices French bread or baguette cut 1-inch thick
- 1 cup of grated Swiss Gruyere and a pinch of Parmesan

Directions:

In a 5 to 6 quart thick-bottomed pot, heat 1 tablespoon of canola oil over medium heat. Add the onions and toss to coat with the canola oil. Cook the onions, stirring often, until they have softened, about 5 to 10 minutes. Increase the heat to medium. Add the remaining tablespoon of canola oil and the butter and cook, stirring often, until the onions start to brown, about 10 more minutes.

Then sprinkle with sugar (to help caramelize) and cook until the onions are well browned, 10 more minutes.

Add the garlic and cook for two minutes.

Add the wine to the pot and scrape up the browned bits on the bottom and sides of the pot, deglazing the pot as you go.

Add the chicken broth, bay leaves, and thyme. Bring to a simmer, cover the pot and lower the heat to maintain a low simmer. Cook for 20 minutes.

Discard the bay leaves. While the soup is simmering, line a sheet pan with parchment paper or foil and preheat the oven to 400°F . Brush both sides of the French bread or baguette slices lightly with butter. Put in the oven and toast until lightly browned, 6 minutes. Remove from the oven. Turn the toast over and sprinkle with the grated Gruyere cheese and Parmesan. Return to the oven when it's close to serving time and bake until the cheese is lightly browned. Remove from the oven. Ladle soup into a bowl and place one cheesy toast on top of each bowl of soup. Add more cheese on top. Enjoy the cheesiness!

Chicken Stew

Ingredients:

- Chicken thighs – for best flavor use *boneless, skinless*
- Canola oil
- Vegetables – *carrots, yellow onion-sauteed , potatoes, frozen peas*
- Garlic
- Chicken broth
- Flour
- Bay leaf – *dried*

Directions:

Set your oven to 375 and cook chicken until brown on all sides, 20 minutes. Take the chicken out of the oven and place on a plate. Cook carrots and onions in a skillet on the stove top, until the onions begin to soften, 4-5 minutes. Add garlic and cook for 3 minute. Add some of the chicken broth, while scraping to loosen browned bits from the bottom. Whisk flour and ¼ cup broth in a small bowl; add to the skillet. Turn the skillet on low. Put chicken on a cutting board and cut chicken into cubes. Put remaining chicken broth, chicken cubes, and ingredients from the skillet into the large pot. Bring to a boil and simmer for 25 minutes over medium-low heat. On a cutting board, cube potatoes. Add potatoes to pot, and cook until potatoes are tender for about 20 minutes. Stir in parsley and discard bay leaf before serving. Serve hot!

Vegetable Soup

Ingredients:

- 3-White potatoes, cut into 1/2-inch cubes
- 3-Carrots- Sliced
- ½ pound of Kale Greens
- 1 can Green beans
- 1-Bell pepper-chopped
- 1 Yellow Onion- Chopped
- 1-Garlic- Minced
- ½ cup of Cauliflower-cut into very small bites
- ½ cup of Broccoli- cut into very small bites
- 1- Can of diced tomatoes
- 1- Zucchini- chopped
- 1 pound of Fresh greens- Kale, collard greens, spinach or mix the greens
- Canola Oil- for the skillet
- Vegetable broth
- 2 cups of Water
- Salt and pepper to taste

Directions:

In a skillet, sauté chopped onion, garlic, carrots, bell pepper in canola oil, with some salt. Add canned diced tomatoes with their juices.
Cook them all together for a couple of minutes. Transfer the ingredients from the skillet to a large pot. Add some vegetable broth, water, salt and

pepper. Add green beans, broccoli, cauliflower and zucchini to the pot. Let cook for 25 minutes. Add chopped greens to the pot and simmer for 5 minutes. Serve hot! Viola!

MAIN DISHES

Roasted Turkey

Ingredients:

4 ounces of butter, melted

Garlic salt

Italian seasoning

10-15 pound turkey (But, this will work with whatever size turley you have).

Directions:

Remove the thawed turkey from it's package. Remove the neck and the bag of giblets Toss them out, (Unless you'd like to make gravy with them later.) Lightly rinse the turkey, under water and pat the turkey dry with paper towels.

Season the outside and cavity of the turkey with garlic salt, and Italian Seasoning.

Tuck the wings of the turkey underneath the turkey, and place in a roasting pan Use your fingers to loosen and lift the skin above the breasts (on the top of the turkey) and smooth a few tablespoons of the seasoning and butter underneath. Use some twine to tie the turkey legs together. Then drench the outside of the turkey with the rest of the butter. Place the turkey in the oven, following the directions of the size of your turkey.

Check the turkey about half way through cooking. (Unless you bought a turkey that has a red, pop-up button).

When the turkey is finished, take the turkey out of the oven, and allow time to cool. About 30-45 minutes. Slice accordingly. Enjoy!

Roasted Salmon

- 2 pound side of boneless, skinless salmon
- 4 sprigs fresh rosemary
- 1 small lemon
- Baking spray
- 2 tablespoons of canola oil (or Extra virgin Olive oil)
- 1 teaspoon of Garlic Salt
- 4 teaspoons of minced garlic
- Chopped fresh Basil

Remove the salmon from the refrigerator and let stand at room temperature for 15 minutes while you prep the other ingredients. Heat oven to 375 degrees F. Line a large rimmed baking sheet with a large piece of aluminum foil. Lightly cover the foil with baking spray. Cut the lemon into thin slices and arrange half of the slices down the middle with the rosemary. Add salmon on top of Rosemary. Drizzle the salmon with the canola oil and sprinkle with the garlic salt. Sprinkle the minced garlic on top. Add the remaining rosemary and lemon slices on top of the salmon.

Fold the sides of the aluminum foil over the top of the salmon until it is completely covered. Bake the salmon for 15-20 minutes, until the salmon is almost completely cooked through. The cooking time will vary based on the thickness of your salmon. Remove the salmon from the oven and carefully open the foil so that the top of the fish is completely uncovered. Change the oven setting to broil, then return the fish to the oven and broil for 5 minutes, until the top of the salmon and the garlic are golden and the fish is cooked thoroughly. Watch the salmon closely, during the broiling process. Remove the salmon from the oven. As soon as it flakes easily with a fork, it's ready.

Cut the salmon into portions. Sprinkle with additional fresh basil or top with an extra squeeze of lemon if you'd like..

Baked Ham

Ingredients:

4-7 lb fully cooked smoked bone-in ham

⅓ cup of honey

⅓ cup packed light brown sugar

4 teaspoons Dijon mustard

Directions:

Heat oven to 375°F. Place ham on the middle rack in a shallow roasting pan. Roast 15 to 20 minutes per pound. Remove ham from the oven. Pour drippings from the roasting pan. Cut the fat off of the ham.

In a small bowl, mix honey, brown sugar and Dijon mustard; brush on the ham. Put the ham back into the oven, uncovered for 30 minutes.Place ham on carving board or platter face down. Using a sharp carving knife, cut next to bone. Cut into slices. Cut remaining slices from the bone-in section, cut away from the bone.

SIDE DISHES

Roasted Garlic Mashed Potatoes

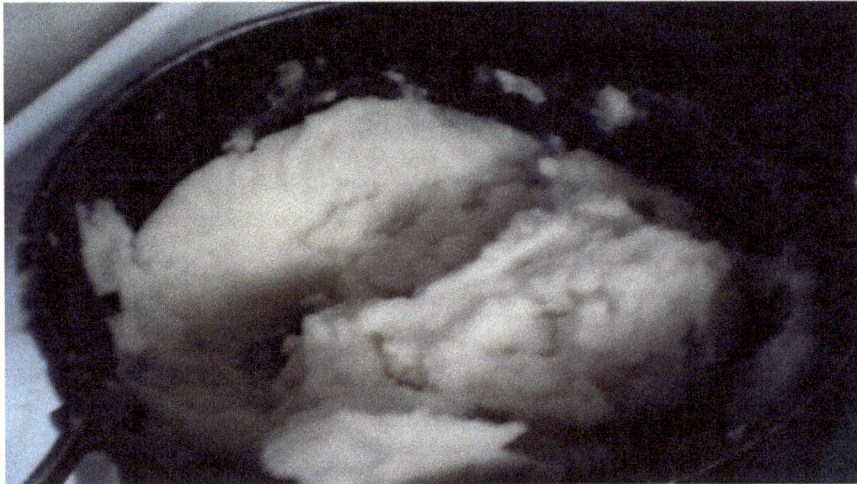

INGREDIENTS

Canola oil, for drizzling

2 tablespoons of minced garlic

4 lb Yellow Yukon potatoes, peeled and chopped

1 stick of butter, melted

2 Pinches of garlic salt

1 c. heavy whipping cream- room temp.

1 teaspoon of Chopped fresh basil, for garnish

Directions:

Preheat the oven to 375°.

Drizzle canola oil over top of garlic and wrap in foil. Bake until golden and soft, 45 minutes. Set aside.

Add potatoes to a large pot. Boil potatoes and season with garlic salt. and season with salt; cover pot and bring to a boil. After about 30 minutes, check to see if the potatoes are soft. Drain the water off of the potatoes.

In a large bowl, mash potatoes. Add butter, cream and garlic. Season with garlic salt and garnish with basil. Serve hot!

Garlic Green Beans

Ingredients:

- 1 pound fresh green beans, trimmed and cut in half
- 4 tablespoons of butter
- 4 teaspoons minced garlic
- Fresh lemon juice
- Pinch of garlic salt

Directions

Place green beans into a large skillet and cover with two cups of water; bring to a boil. Reduce heat to medium and simmer for 5 minutes. Drain water. Add butter to the skillet, and cook and stir until butter is melted for 2 minutes. Cook and stir garlic with green beans until garlic is tender and fragrant, 4 minutes. Season with garlic salt. Before serving, splash fresh lemon juice on green beans. Serve warm.

GREENS AND BEANS

Ingredients:

- 3 Heads of Kale
- ⅓ cup of extra virgin olive oil
- 2 teaspoons of minced garlic
- 1 (15 ounce) can cannellini beans, drained and rinsed
- 2 Tablespoons of fresh parmesan cheese

Directions:

In a large pot, bring ½ cup of water to a boil. Add kale. Cook the kale at a boil, for 5 minutes; drain.

Pour EVOO into the pot and place over medium heat. Cook and stir in garlic. Simmer for 5 minutes. Stir drained kale and cannellini beans into the garlic mixture; cook and stir until the beans are hot- 7 minutes. Sprinkle Parmesan cheese over the mixture just before serving. Serve warm.

Holiday Desserts

Christmas Sugar Cookies

- 2 ¾ cups all-purpose flour

- 1 teaspoon baking soda

- ½ teaspoon baking powder

- 1 cup butter, softened

- 1 ½ cups white sugar

- 1 egg

- 1 teaspoon vanilla extract

- **Step 1**

  Preheat the oven to 365 degrees F. In a small bowl, stir together flour, baking soda, and baking powder. Set aside.

- **Step 2**

  In a big bowl, mix together the butter and sugar until smooth. Mix in the egg and vanilla. Mix in the dry ingredients. Roll teaspoonfuls of dough into balls, and place onto lightly greased cookie sheet.

- **Step 3**

  Bake for 10 minutes in the preheated oven, or until golden brown. Let cool. Then, take off of the cookie sheet and serve.

Holiday Rum Balls

INGREDIENTS

- 4 cups of crushed vanilla wafers
- 1 cup of confectioners' sugar
- ⅓ cup unsweetened cocoa powder
- 1 ⅓ cups finely chopped pecans
- 2 teaspoon2 pure vanilla extract
- 4 tablespoons corn syrup
- ¾ cup of rum (any rum you like!)

INSTRUCTIONS

In a large bowl, stir together the crushed vanilla wafers, 1 cup of confectioners' sugar, cocoa, and pecans. Add in vanilla, corn syrup and rum. Shape the dough mixture into 1 inch balls.

Roll Rum Balls in additional confectioners' sugar, cocoa, and leftover ingredients. Store in an airtight container and place in the refrigerator for several days to get the strongest flavor, before serving.

Sugarplums

Ingredients:

1 cup chopped pitted dates

1 cup chopped walnuts

¾ cup dried cranberries

¾ cup chopped prunes

¾ cup chopped hazelnuts

3 tablespoons plum or fruit preserves

⅓ teaspoon ground cinnamon

⅓ teaspoon nutmeg

¾ cup sugar

Directions:

Place the chopped dates, prunes, cranberries, hazelnuts, and walnuts in a food processor . Pulse the mixture for 8 times. Add the fruit preserves, cinnamon and cloves, and pulse until the mixture begins to come together. Do **NOT** overprocess it into a paste. Roll the candy into small 1-inch balls. Then roll into the sugar until they are fully covered. Store the finished sugarplums in an airtight container between layers of waxed paper until you serve them. Yummy!

Thank you so much for your support!
Have a blessed and wonderful Holiday
Season!